Negotiating Techniques in Diplomacy and Business Contracts

Charles Chatterjee

Negotiating Techniques in Diplomacy and Business Contracts

palgrave
macmillan

Charles Chatterjee
Institute of Advanced Legal Studies
University of London
London, UK

ISBN 978-3-030-81731-2 ISBN 978-3-030-81732-9 (eBook)
https://doi.org/10.1007/978-3-030-81732-9

This Palgrave Macmillan imprint is published by the registered company Springer Nature Switzerland AG.
The registered company address is: Gewerbestrasse 11, 6330 Cham, Switzerland

The opinions expressed in this book are those of the author, and in no way may be attributed to the institution to which he belongs.

Contents

About the Author

Charles Chatterjee is Associate Research Fellow at the Institute of Advanced Legal Studies, University of London, UK. He has published books and articles on a variety of topics including diplomacy, private foreign investments, dispute settlement, banking, import-export trade, public international law and other related topics.

CHAPTER 1

Introduction

The primary objectives of this work are twofold: to emphasise (a) how good negotiating techniques may lead contracts or agreements of all nature to the satisfaction of all parties concerned, and (b) what kind of expertise diplomats and commercial negotiators should possess in achieving satisfactory agreements. This work has also dealt with the issues of the knowledge, expertise and interactive capacity of diplomats and commercial negotiators in successfully negotiating diplomatic and business deals. It has also emphasised the role of women in effective negotiations of both diplomatic and commercial matters.

This work has been developed over eight chapters:

Chapter 2: Negotiating Techniques in Diplomacy
Chapter 3: Negotiating Techniques in Concluding Business Contracts
Chapter 4: Women's Role in Negotiating Diplomatic and Business Deals
Chapter 5: Negotiating Techniques in Import-Export Trade
Chapter 6: Negotiating Techniques in Ending Armed Conflicts
Chapter 7: Negotiating Techniques in Arranging Project Finance and Syndicated Loan Agreements
Chapter 8: The United Nations System and Diplomacy
Chapter 9: Conclusions

In regard to negotiating techniques in relation to economic diplomacy, it is re-iterated that economic diplomacy is wider in scope than

C. Chatterjee, *Negotiating Techniques in Diplomacy and Business Contracts*, https://doi.org/10.1007/978-3-030-81732-9_1

commercial diplomacy; however, whereas economic diplomacy is primarily concerned with policy-making for the home country vis-à-vis other countries, particularly with a view to formulating economic policies, commercial diplomacy is part of economic diplomacy. Foreign policy-making is very much based on two important issues: (a) how should the government of a country be engaged in creating future business prospects with other countries including investment and security issues; and (b) good inter-State relationship easily establishes rapport between them even in regard to defence-related issues. Hence it is maintained that economic diplomacy to a large extent forms the basis for foreign policy-making too.[1]

Economic diplomacy's objectives and scope of activities may be clearly identified by remembering that it really is an important kind of diplomacy *sui generis* than commercial diplomacy although these two forms of diplomacy have been used by certain authors interchangeably,[2] which should not really be the case. On the other hand, the interplay between economic diplomacy and foreign policy-making has become intertwined.[3] Whereas commercial diplomacy has a business tone, in addition to being a vehicle for foreign policy-making, economic diplomacy has a broader base; it is also a factor of foreign policy-making of a State.

The controversy surrounding the interchangeability of the terms, commercial diplomacy and economic diplomacy seems to be never-ending. According to Ruel, commercial diplomacy develops international relations for businesses;[4] however, Narang believes that commercial diplomacy is a vital component of economic diplomacy.[5]

This author maintains that economic diplomacy is not exclusively concerned with profit-making when interacting with other States; it also aims at developing rules of behaviour of States particularly at a diplomatic level. In addition to developing commercial rapport, representatives of States also negotiate treaties one of the objectives of which is to strengthen the rapport between the States in mutual interests.

[1] See further C Chatterjee, *Economic Diplomacy and Foreign Policy-Making*, New York and Switzerland, Palgrave Macmillan (2020).

[2] G Pigman, *Contemporary Diplomacy*, Cambridge, Polity Press (2010).

[3] K S Rana, *21st Century Diplomacy*, The Continuum International Publishing Group (2011); see also C Chatterjee, op. cit., at p V.

[4] H Ruel, *Commercial Diplomacy and International Business: A Conceptual and Empirical Exploration*, Emerald Group (2012).

[5] O Narang, *Commercial Diplomacy: A Conceptual Overview: A Paper presented to the 7th World Conference of TPOS*, The Hague (2008).

Controversies aside, in order to satisfy all concerned, one should consider the following in the main:

- The real forms of economic diplomacy and foreign policy-making;
- The tenets of economic diplomacy;
- Economic diplomacy and commercial diplomacy;
- Emerging markets and changing patterns of economic diplomacy;
- Negotiating techniques in economic diplomacy;
- Economic diplomacy at international fora;
- Economic diplomacy and negotiation of economic treaties including private foreign investment treaties;
- Developing countries and economic diplomacy; and
- The role of non-governmental institutions in economic diplomacy.

The importance of effective negotiations in both economic and commercial diplomatic matters may not be denied. It is for this reason that the qualities of a good negotiator have also been identified in this work. The traditional view that higher bargaining power of a party will win its case in any of the afore-mentioned fields is over. Developing countries, in general, are also changing their traditional views on private foreign investments, import-export trade, manufacturing and agricultural activities.

Furthermore, they have been gradually developing their own ideas about exploitation of their own very large human resources in addition to their natural resources. They should also quickly learn how to negotiate with the other parties on an equal footing.

Finally, with the fast-changing world particularly with the aid of technology, time has now arrived for developing and middle-grade countries to change their strategies in regard to cross-border business projects and in the diplomatic world too. It is with this hope and belief that this book has been developed.

In writing this book, primary sources of information have been relied upon, where possible. Secondary sources of information have been referred to, where necessary.

This work has been addressed to practising diplomats, commercial negotiators and post-graduate students.

CHAPTER 2

Negotiating Techniques in Diplomacy

2.1 Introduction

Negotiating techniques in diplomacy and those in the commercial world would be different, as the subject matters of negotiations are different. However, the qualities of a diplomat and those of a commercial negotiator would be similar. All diplomats, irrespective of their grades, are required to possess knowledge and expertise in negotiating techniques. In diplomatic studies, training in negotiating techniques is not usually accorded much importance simply because in the diplomatic world there exists a strong belief that diplomats need not require special training in negotiating techniques, which may not necessarily be true. Negotiation is an inevitable phenomenon at almost all stages of a diplomat's work. Hence it is important for diplomats to formally go through a learning process to become competent negotiators.

In this chapter an attempt has been made to explain what negotiating techniques really stands for and how mastery over them may be attained by diplomats. In negotiating any deal with a counterpart, a diplomat must remember that he/she must achieve what his/her Foreign Office wants him/her to achieve through negotiations.

C. Chatterjee, *Negotiating Techniques in Diplomacy and Business Contracts*, https://doi.org/10.1007/978-3-030-81732-9_2

2.2 What Is Meant by Negotiation and the Qualities that a Negotiator Should Possess

2.2.1 *What Is Negotiation?*

It may be defined as a process to reach a compromised decision which would serve the purposes of both the parties for which they decided to negotiate. In a negotiating process both the parties hold equal position. It is misleading to think that a higher bargaining power would have more influence; this kind of view of negotiation should not be taken seriously. The Concise Oxford English Dictionary defines "bargaining power" as the "power to negotiate."[1] The reader is politely reminded that the old-fashioned idea that negotiators from the Western part of the world, by virtue of their being industrialised and wealthier than the countries in the poor world, will have more bargaining power than the negotiators belonging to the poor world, is no longer true. Diplomats from developing countries should prepare themselves very thoroughly with their strategies and policies. More of this has received attention in the next section of this chapter.

2.2.2 *The Formalities of Negotiating Techniques in Diplomacy*

The discipline of "diplomacy" is multi-dimensional; thus diplomats must learn negotiating techniques in various aspects of diplomacy: general diplomacy, economic diplomacy, commercial diplomacy, trade diplomacy and investment diplomacy, war diplomacy, environmental diplomacy and so on. When a diplomat may be engaged in any type of the abovementioned diplomacy, he/she must do and remember two things—(a) his/her own strategy and demands and (b) other side's strategies and demands—and thereafter find the grounds for compromise through negotiations.

What should a diplomat do at a negotiation session? First, he/she must be smartly dressed; the national dress will also do. If any party to a negotiation session requires any translator, it is for the party at whose location the negotiation would take place to provide it, although the use of the same language by both the parties would be better and less time-consuming.

[1] *Concise Oxford English Dictionary*, Oxford, Clarendon Press (1990) at 132.

Second, each member of the negotiating teams must introduce himself/herself briefly and clearly. Incidentally, it is always useful to include female members in a negotiating team. The oral expressions made during a negotiation process must be simple; members of the teams must not use any ambiguous terms during a negotiation process. They must exchange their business cards with their counterparts. There should be an agreed agenda for each session if, of course, the negotiation requires more than one session. Body language should be avoided, as such language may be misinterpreted by certain members of the teams or it may offend the members of the other side.

Third, each party to a negotiation session must appoint a leader who should be very familiar with the subject matter for which negotiations are being held, and whose function would also be to ensure an orderly negotiation process. In the event of any stalemate occurring during a negotiation process, it is for the leaders to give a break to the negotiation session, and to discuss the points of discontent; thereafter the proposed solution should be put to the members of the negotiating teams to ascertain their collective views.

Fourth, in the event of the collective views of the two teams being significantly different, a further cooling-off period should be allowed for a further reflection process, and then meet again perhaps on the following day. It is important to ensure that no negotiation process fails as otherwise its consequences would be disastrous.

Fifth, socialisation should be within permissible limits bearing in mind that in many countries over-socialisation, particularly with the female members of the teams or with the females of the local community, is often a taboo, and it can bring a negotiation process to a sudden halt.

Sixth, no party to a negotiation process must make any adverse comments on each other's country; on the contrary, each party's members should provide some of the good features and qualities of the other party's country.

Seventh, throughout the entire negotiation process, diplomats from both sides must remain courteous, polite and must not display their dissatisfaction in any way. It is important to bear in mind that once negotiation process is disturbed for whatever reason, it will result in nothing. It is also important to bear in mind that negotiation is the best way of resolving disputes on any issue between the two parties.

Eighth, the members of the teams on each side must be chosen in a way that it includes diplomats each of whom will have special expertise in certain issues which have arisen out of the dispute. A dispute is often multi-dimensional.

Ninth, in a no-alcohol-drinking society, after the day's session is over, the members of the team wishing to drink alcohol should first seek the permission from the leader of the home country team, otherwise the home country's team may feel offended, and this will have an adverse impact on the negotiation process as from the next day.

Tenth, the members of the participating teams should exchange their *curriculum vitae* a few days before the actual negotiation session takes place.

Eleventh, all members of the negotiating teams should be familiar with the basic information of the other team's country profile, which may be obtained from the World Bank's (International Bank for Reconstruction and Development—IBRD) website.

Twelfth, finally, after the negotiation process is over, the parties should exchange gifts (souvenirs) between themselves as a gesture of friendship. This duty should be performed by the leader of each team.

In writing these items, no particular order has been maintained as it was not found necessary to do so.

2.3 Preparations for Negotiations

This is the most difficult stage to complete in order to ensure that the final negotiation process becomes successful. Without a knowledge in the country profile, and more importantly, the nature of the dispute or difference between the parties, no negotiation process may lead to any success. Incidentally, what most people call a "dispute" in reality is a "difference" of views on the same issue(s) between the parties concerned. A "dispute" is a legal term, which is concerned with the legal rights and remedies of a party or of both the parties concerned. Therefore, it is of utmost importance for the parties to determine what they are about to "negotiate" is a "dispute" or "difference" of views on the same issue(s) held by each party.

Once the abovementioned issue has been determined, each member of the team must familiarise himself/herself with the nature of the issue(s) and the causes thereof. Unless the causes of the differences between the parties have been identified, no effective negotiation may take place. Again, if the causes of differences or of a dispute between the parties have been identified, then each member should go into the historical reasons for the causes arising for the differences/disputes between the parties. The leader of each team must be thoroughly involved in this exercise, and where necessary, documentary evidence in support of any argument that a member of a team may put forward would be very useful.

Mock sessions as a preliminary to an actual negotiation session are often found useful; these sessions also provide opportunities to learn the weaknesses in an argument, and on the basis of that experience, members of a team should correct their arguments or certain issues. Here, the leader of a team has to take a real lead on this matter. After the mock sessions have taken place, each member of a team should prepare his/her dossier on the issue(s) in which an actual negotiating session would be involved.

During the preparation stage, each party should carefully determine its strategies and develop its arguments accordingly. Members of a team should be prepared to accept the other side's valid arguments on certain issue(s); by the same token, where necessary, they should also demonstrate their opposition to certain arguments which may be put forward by the other side, politely and not in an offensive fashion.

In selecting members of a negotiating team, the leader of the team should ensure that each member of it is highly qualified in the issues which would be the subject matter for an actual negotiation process. He/she must also ensure that no member of his/her team is short-tempered as such a member might spoil the actual negotiation process.

Each member of a team should demonstrate his/her willingness to settle the difference/dispute between the parties on the issue(s) with which a negotiating process would be concerned.

Where it would be appropriate to refer to the established principles of international law, including the customary rules of international law, each party should draw the attention of the other party to it.

2.4 Costs of Negotiation

It is for the receiving State to arrange accommodation for the stay of the guests in the country, although the accommodation costs are usually borne by the guest party; however, the costs of lunches, dinners, teas and/or coffees are to be paid for by the receiving State. Usually, the receiving State also arranges transport both ways from the guests' accommodation to the venue of negotiation sessions. Of course, other incidental expenses such as photocopying of documents are usually covered by the receiving State. On a future occasion, the sending State would be obliged to pay similar expenses when the receiving state's delegates would be visiting the sending State on similar occasions.

2.5 The Time Lag Between Preparations and the Final Session of a Negotiating Process

The time lag between the preparatory sessions and the final session of negotiation(s) should be described as the time for reflection to determine the prospects of winning at the actual session(s). By that time, both the parties must have accepted their proposals for negotiation. During the "time lag" both parties should once again examine the strategies and plans for negotiating the differences between them. In conducting negotiation sessions each party should study the strategies and tactics on which the other party might rely. After perusing the proposal for negotiation received from the other side and after holding the preparatory sessions, the parties may have to change their strategies; thus, the areas of disagreement should be minimised in order to ensure that the final negotiation sessions would bring the differences between the parties to a successful end. Incidentally, there does not exist any objections to changing the strategies of the parties, as strategies are never disclosed to any third party. It is to be emphasised that it is the quality of the arguments and friendliness on the part of the members of a negotiating team that matter most.

The "reflection time" is also important for the leaders of teams. They should be able to brief their members of the respective teams in a more effective way. Therefore, this interregnum should be utilised in a profitable manner. It is for the leader to provide new ideas, if any, to the members of the team, and give his/her opinions on them.

Members of each team can also do their own research on the contentious issues during the "reflection time" and raise some valuable questions which should alert the members of both the teams during the actual negotiating sessions. In a negotiating process certain issues raised by the members of one side might annoy the members of the other party which should be avoided, and everybody at the negotiating sessions must remain calm and patient.

2.6 The Negotiation Process

There are certain formalities that each member of the negotiating teams must observe and the leaders too. It is for the leader of the home (receiving State) team to welcome the foreign team, and introduce himself/herself first, and the leader of the guest party will do the same.

After that each of the members of the home team should introduce themselves, and thereafter, the foreign party's members should also do the same. Each member of the teams should display his/her name on cards in front of them. Members of each of the teams must pronounce each member's name correctly. Unless so permitted by each member, members of the teams should not address any member by his/her first name. This is a matter of courtesy which a party expects of the other party. Throughout a negotiation process, each member must remain courteous and display good manners. After both parties have completed what may be described as the "introduction" session, the real work usually starts. Incidentally, all members of the teams, male and female, must be addressed correctly and politely.

The real business, the negotiation process will start then. By this time, the members of both the teams should be familiar with their mandates; in the case of any difficulties they should ask their leaders for assistance. However, at the initial stage, it is for the leader of each team to summarise briefly the nature of the differences or disputes between the two parties (each of the parties will represent its own country). Usually, the contracting party (the party that initiates to negotiate the differences between the parties) opens the negotiation process after summarising the nature of the difference/dispute in regard to a matter on which the two parties have decided to negotiate.

After the negotiation process has commenced, the leader of the party may advise the relevant member of the party to present his/her contention on behalf of his/her country before the negotiating session. Then, of course, his/her counterpart will respond to that contention. This process will be observed throughout the negotiation process, and hopefully, they will eventually narrow down their differences and bring about a solution to the problem. Of course, best negotiations take place during tea or coffee breaks, that is, in an informal way, but the result of the informal negotiation can be formalised at a negotiation meeting.

After a negotiation process has successfully completed a joint report in an agreed language should be drafted in a simple way, and the heads of the foreign offices of both the parties must sign it to formalise the negotiated solution to the differences between the two governments, and exchange the copies of it between the foreign offices of the parties concerned.

Once again, it is not by instructions only that command in negotiating techniques may be developed in an individual. Often negotiating techniques need a personal contribution but within limits. Thus, prior to commencing any diplomatic negotiation process, a mandate from the foreign office should be obtained, which should contain a degree of flexibility which would allow the negotiators to do a degree of manoeuvre during the negotiation process.

Negotiators must have a high sense of perseverance to ensure that the process comes to a fruition, as it is important to bear in mind that if a negotiation process should fail, the parties will be left with no choice but to settle their disputes through court proceedings or conciliation or by arbitration, each of which procedures entails high costs and time.

It would be advisable to take an appropriate advantage to negotiate the parties' utmost. Sometimes it proves to be helpful to start with the historical friendship between the countries concerned.

2.7 Negotiating Techniques in War Diplomacy

Negotiating techniques in resolving inter-State or multi-State disputes or differences should be a compulsory part of briefing of diplomats at all foreign offices. Techniques of developing foreign relations and economic diplomacy will continue to change. Thus the techniques of negotiating all forms of diplomacy, trade, environment, health, education and, of course, war diplomacy should be learned by diplomats. This section of this chapter has been solely allocated to war diplomacy.

The reader is reminded very briefly of the deplorable history of humankind which is full of warfares right from the beginning of the communities of humankind. During the early years of the international community, at least until the beginning of the First World War in 1914, warfares were not really based on deadly technology. Nevertheless, the fact remains that the older societies even if engaged in primitive forms of war were engaged in warfares, based on various reasons. But however primitive the form of the war was, all wars killed people indiscriminately. When the use of rather sophisticated weapons became common, particularly since the First World War more deadly weapons have been used, in addition to deadly skirmishes between people, the consequential effect to the countries have been depicted and remembered in history. The first attempt to abolish warfares was made by the League of Nations through its Covenant, Article 15(2) which, in particular, provided that:

> ... the parties to the dispute will communicate to the Secretary-General, as promptly as possible, statements of their case with all the relevant facts and papers, and the Council may forthwith direct publication thereof.

Then the entire world experienced the deadly Second World War which lasted for six years and literally devastated many parts of the world. The United Nations was established on 24 October 1945. Its Charter was a very thoughtful document; the primary objectives were many, but briefly, to abolish warfare, to provide guidelines to the UN Members to enable them to achieve socio-economic development, rights and freedoms of people, to name but a few. Unfortunately, the majority of the Member States of the United Nations tend to disregard the guidelines that the agencies of it or of the UN itself renders whether in the form of Conventions, Resolutions or Declarations or Charter unless some of them have already developed customary norms of international law, which are then treated to be binding. Article 2, paragraph 4, of the UN Charter provides that:

> All Members shall refrain in their international relations from the threat or use of force against the territorial integrity or political independence of any State, or in any other manner inconsistent with the Purposes of the United Nations.

Sadly again, over the past few years, the international community has been witnessing too many warfares, for example, the attack on Iraq by the UK and US, the war between Saudi Arabia and Yemen, the war within Syria, the Kashmir (in India) problem, the Arab-Israeli conflict, the war between Russia and Ukraine, to name but a few. In addition to causing environmental problems, each of these wars has caused untold human miseries; the victims of these warfares are in most cases refugees, children's lives, including their deteriorating health conditions, no opportunities to gain basic education, terrible poverty and diseases; these are not only their problems, but the entire international community is now required to pay attention to their conditions.

A number of non-governmental organisations, including the International Red Cross, have been doing their best under their individual mandates, but they alone cannot rehabilitate the refugees. These acts do not come under Article 2, paragraph 7, even if their consequences adversely affect the international community. Article 2, paragraph 7, provides that:

> Nothing contained in the present Charter shall authorise the United Nations to intervene in matters which are essentially within the domestic jurisdiction of any State or shall require the Members to submit such matters to settlement under the present Charter; but this principle shall not prejudice the application of enforcement measures under Chapter VII.

The question remains that although apparently their acts may appear to come under the purview of Article 2, paragraph 7, in reality, they do not do so, as the provisions of this paragraph (paragraph 7) must be read with those of paragraph 4 of Article 2 of the UN Charter. The country that attacks the peoples within their boundaries or foreign countries is in breach of the principle of State Responsibility of international law, and it is also in breach of the Responsibility to Protect the people within their jurisdiction. Alternatively, if they have shown their atrocities towards the refugees or foreigners residing within their jurisdiction, then also they may be accused of criminal acts by making people subject to immeasurable human sufferings. In the event of their attempts to resolve this issue by discussing this matter with the State from which they originated, having failed, the matter should have been referred to the United Nations; furthermore, no foreign State should be allowed to provide weapons or other forms of assistance to the country that should be accused of causing human miseries. War begets war, hence the need for diplomatic negotiations.

Initially, diplomatic negotiations should take place between the home country and the country from which the refugees have entered into the home country; if that should not succeed such a matter should be referred to a conciliation procedure, and if this second option should also fail, then the matter should be referred to the appropriate Committee or Commission of the United Nations, rather than people suffering from immeasurable miseries. At the UN forum, both parties should agree to express their genuine options and let the Committee or Commission decide on it, and their decision should be communicated to the Office of the UN Secretary-General with a request to send its opinion to the home country concerned, rather than allowing any other country to intervene in that country's matter even though the home country may have requested the latter to intervene. In fact, from a legal standpoint, the third country, even though invited by the home country, should not have intervened in the first place or provided the home country with assistance, be it financial or even supplying weapons.

Diplomats should appreciate that any breach of the UN Charter provisions by them simply invites criticisms from the law-abiding States and sets bad examples. Days of diplomacy are changing fast and they are now experiencing novel problems for which there may not be any precedents. Furthermore, peoples' voices need to be heard in the contemporary period; dictatorial heads of States may not govern their country for a long time, although there do exist a few dictatorial States, which are primarily governed by Marxism.

Historically, at least over the past two or three decades, the incidence of diplomacy in settling disputes/differences be they bilateral or multilateral has not been used that often, and when used, has proved to be unsuccessful.

The diplomatic world is now required to reflect on the efficacy of the traditional diplomacy to cope with the demands of novel situations.

2.8 Why Should Contemporary Diplomats Be Required to Be More Dynamic Than Ever Before?

Diplomats in the contemporary world are required to think of the various dimensions to each of the current topics in relation to which they may be required to negotiate. For example, wars present multi-dimensional problems. The adverse effect of warfares need not be discussed and negotiated in isolation, for while negotiating a warfare for ceasing it, the diplomats, as negotiators, would be required to deal with issues such as the environment, rehabilitation of refugees, treatment of the wounded among others.

Behind each warfare in the contemporary period, there exist vocal oppositions by many societies; the parties who wage warfare these days should not really disregard the voices of discontent. Furthermore, under the UN Charter, warfares are prohibited as is the use of force.

This work emphasises the importance of utilising the United Nations, as it is currently the most accessible international forum, but unfortunately, this forum remains under-utilised in many ways.

Racial hatred has proved to be one of the most important factors of warfare between the races concerned—this should not be a cause of warfare. Interesting to note that this type of hatred is no longer confined to black and white people, people practising different religions, but bearing similar complexions, have become victims of racial discrimination which has caused warfares, the direct consequence of which have become immeasurable miseries to human beings and the number of refugees has gone up by leaps and bounds, poverty has increased and human resources are not being utilised. This is an issue which should be regarded as a matter of "international concern" and deserves attention of the United Nations, and the entire world community, including their diplomats or representatives to formulate policies for stopping such warfares rather than relying on baseless justification that these are issues of domestic jurisdiction.

Racial hatred originates from prejudices which may be avoided by heightening the level of public awareness. Higher education may not provide remedies against prejudices or prevent prejudices. If only the Members of the United Nations were sufficiently united on such issues, perhaps many of the current problems could have been avoided.

This is a matter on which high level of awareness among States, Members of the United Nations, would be urgently needed.

2.9 The Importance of Peace-Making Diplomacy

As long as racial discrimination would be practised, warfares would remain a common phenomenon in the world. There can be other causes of warfares too, but the above statement is made on the basis of the recent warfares in Africa and Asia and the Middle East. One of the means of resolving this problem would be to enact legislation to prohibit it provided, of course, appropriate enforcement measures of the legislation are also in place.

Whereas warfares directly indicate hatred of one class of people towards another, and their ultimate effect would be costs, creation of refugees, damage to the environment, adverse downturn to economies and its consequential effect; peace-making does not cost anybody anything; it is a question of ascertaining the strategies as to how to develop it. Furthermore, successful peace-deals develop friendly relations between countries and the people therein.

There are various means of developing peace between and among the States—mutual trade, tourism, exchange of educational opportunities, and even exchange of cultural events between States. Diplomats require special training as to how to form the foundations of mutual peace-making and to familiarise themselves with the ingredients of peace-making. Dependence of countries on mutual trade, including shipping and joint economic programmes between them, should be a certain means of developing peace in the participating States.

If peace diplomacy can set good examples of resolution of differences between parties, then war diplomacy may not be needed as the ultimate aim of the former is to bring an end to warfares and return to peace.

One should take the example of Europe in order to reaffirm how mutual trade between States can be a peace-making factor. The Victory in Europe Day was 8 May 1945 whereby entire Western Europe and the UK were freed from Nazism. Indeed, the surrender by Germany was obtained through negotiations between Churchill, then prime minister of Great Britain, and Adolf Hitler. As stated earlier that no responsible and sensible country would like to jeopardise her trade relationships with other countries; protection and preservation of this relationship provide peace also. It has also been stated in this work that trade forms the basis for foreign policy-making of countries too.

It is rather interesting to note that some of the States seem to be taking a rather long time to appreciate the miseries that warfares bring with them, and both the UN aid agencies and various non-governmental organisations are required to extend help and even aid as much as possible; even States are required to help the victims of warfares, when necessary, and all this, when reflected upon, should appear to be unnecessary. It is elementary to realise that warfares are instrumental to making enemies, and by drawing analogies with practical aspects of life, it may be maintained that no two human beings are same; no two nations, let alone States, may be expected to think alike and behave themselves in a similar way. Yet, warfares go on primarily, as explained in this section, on the basis of prejudices against others. The equation is rather simple—if peace diplomacy fails, the international community is left with nothing as the primary objective of war diplomacy is to ensure that warfares come to an end, but unfortunately, the success rate of such diplomacy is not very high. Hence, the suggestions that perhaps the non-parties to a warfare should take the initiative to refer warfares initially to the UN General Assembly, and thereafter to the Security Council asking them to end them and make arrangements for a settlement of the dispute under the Chairmanship of the Secretary-General of the UN, or any other competent officer to be deputised by him.

Furthermore, Article 33 of the UN Charter provides that:

1. The parties to any dispute, the continuance of which is likely to endanger the maintenance of international peace and security, shall, first of all seek a solution by negotiation, enquiry, mediation, conciliation, arbitration, judicial settlement, resort to regional agencies or arrangements, or other peaceful means of their own choice.
2. The Security Council shall, when it deems necessary, call upon the parties to settle their dispute by such means.

Third-party diplomats may also draw the attention of the heads of State/Foreign Offices of the parties engaged in warfares to exhaust paragraph 1 of Article 33, in particular, negotiation, conciliation or judicial settlement or any other peaceful means of their own choice to bring the warfares to a close. They should be in close touch with the Security Council of the UN in order to enable the Council to take measures under paragraph 2 of Article 33.

2.10 Conclusions

Peace diplomacy may be described as a "limitless" diplomacy; diplomats engaged in peace diplomacy should not only have good skills in negotiating techniques but also be familiar with the art of convincing the parties engaged in warfares, the far-reaching adverse effects of their warfares and related activities.

In the contemporary world, peoples' aspirations have changed; warfares are disliked by most people and yet majority of the States still seem to remain indifferent to the major issues which hinder the progress of this world. High level of public awareness of the apparent reasons which cause warfares and racial hatred is essential. Peace diplomacy should be a good means of eradicating these two known causes by drawing attention of the public at various international fora.

CHAPTER 3

Negotiating Techniques in Concluding Business Contracts

3.1 Introduction

In the diplomatic world there exists a general belief that diplomats know how to negotiate various issues either on a bilateral or on a multilateral basis, but this may not be entirely true, bearing in mind that the world politics is changing very fast indeed. The major players in the world of diplomacy are diplomats of all categories and the Foreign Office delegates in whatever name they may be described (e.g. US Department of State). In this continuously changing world it is clear that diplomats of all categories are required to learn diplomacy with its new dimensions in order to ensure that they are sufficiently advanced in diplomacy, be it in relation to trade, investment, development, wars and peace, to be able to present their views articulately but not to suit exclusively their governments, but to suit the international community, where needed.

Furthermore, diplomats should also appreciate that their expertise does not necessarily and solely relate to their knowledge in international relations; they are also required to possess some essential knowledge in public international law, otherwise, most of the negotiations may end in failures.

Diplomats' selection procedure needs to be reviewed and reconsidered by many States. In addition to their hands-on experience, they should be subject to what is popularly known as Continuing Professional Development (CPD), by holding special capacity-building sessions by

C. Chatterjee, *Negotiating Techniques in Diplomacy and Business Contracts*, https://doi.org/10.1007/978-3-030-81732-9_3

external experts with considerable knowledge in diplomacy and diplomatic negotiations.

Diplomats have two most important functions to discharge, among others. They must protect their core national interests, particularly from a security point of view, as they must have a thorough knowledge in how to present their special cases before the United Nations and its Specialised agencies, in particular, the International Labour Organisation (ILO), World Health Organization (WHO), World Trade Organization (WTO), UN Development Programmes Office (UNDP), UN Conference on Trade and Development (UNCTAD) and International Maritime Organisation (IMO), to name but a few.

Most of all, diplomats of all categories must have competence in negotiating techniques in all aspects of the important issues, namely, trade, private foreign investments, war and peace, sea-related issues, the issues relating to environmental and climate change, women's rights and so on. These issues should not be left to their lawyers, whose services may be needed for drafting the negotiated or conciliated results.

Diplomats should bear in mind that at all negotiating sessions the less powerful States will always encounter vehement opposition on certain issues from the more powerful States, be they powerful from an economic or a financial point of view or militarily. They must also have special expertise in negotiating peace than wars; the demerits of warfares need not be discussed in this context.

Rather than holding a rigid sense of sovereignty in respect of all issues and matters, diplomats should take the initiative to negotiate or conciliate on them where possible. By the same token, rather than holding an adverse view of the United Nations, they should appropriately utilise the international platforms, where possible, and correct the organisation's approaches on issues and matters, where necessary.

There does not exist any published works on these aspects of diplomacy; this author in 2000 published a work[1] on negotiating techniques primarily in regard to commercial contracts. That work did not contain any discussion of the principal themes of this current work. In the absence of many primary sources of information, this work had to refer to secondary sources of information—published works and in certain cases, legislation.

[1] C Chatterjee, *Negotiating Techniques in International Commercial Contracts*, Aldershot, Ashgate (2000).

3.2 Who Should Be a Diplomat?

The term diplomacy, according to the Oxford Dictionary of English, has been defined as

> the profession, activity or skill of managing international relations, typically by a country's representatives abroad.[2]

It may also be defined as:

> the art of management of relationships between countries.

If these two definitions are combined, the following traits of "diplomacy" may be discerned.

(a) That, it is a profession, which implies that a diplomat is supposed to display "professionalism" which usually requires him/her to possess a thorough knowledge of his/her profession. Thus, all diplomats, male or female, are required to go through the profession of diplomacy, in the form of training and education, in order to achieve competence in conducting diplomacy in this very fast-changing world;[3]
(b) The question remains how many States in reality give their diplomats the thorough training and education they require in the contemporary period? It may sound to be a rather unkind question, but the fact remains that when diplomacy started a few centuries ago, it was in its rudimentary stage. The family background of diplomats matters most in electing and selecting them for their appointment. Even the nature of economic diplomacy, which was primarily concerned with import/export trade and general diplomatic relations between two jurisdictions, has changed. The choice of these jurisdictions was primarily based on mutual economic benefits. One is required to remember that currencies were not devised by any nation in the olden days; thus their trade was primarily based on a countertrade or barter system. Interestingly enough, these methods of payment have returned as methods of payment when governments or public bodies are buyers and sellers. This is another issue with which diplomats engaged in promoting import-export trade should be familiar. These methods of

[2] Oxford, Oxford University Press at 494.
[3] See further G R Berridge, *Diplomacy, Theory and Practice, Part I, The Art of Negotiation*, New York, Palgrave Macmillan (2010).

payment do not strain the foreign exchange deposits of the two jurisdictions concerned;

(c) A diplomat should be a multi-lingual person. Although traditionally, in the diplomatic world, many still seem to hold the view that French is the most popular language for diplomats, the English language seems to have taken over the French language. Indeed, the French language has dominated the diplomatic world until recently; it has become apparent particularly over the past decade or so that the English language has taken over the French language in carrying out diplomatic activities between and among the States. Thus, in addition to mastering one language for diplomatic work, diplomats will have privilege if they were multi-lingual. However, he/she must be articulate in the language he/she may have chosen to communicate with others;

(d) A diplomat must be familiar with the universally accepted manners and etiquettes, although greetings at the first meeting with the other diplomats in his/her "national way" would not do any harm. The language of a diplomat should be simple so that his/her counterpart experiences no difficulty in understanding it. Diplomats must be well dressed. They can also wear their national dress. Appearance in its totality matters. Many may find casual dress offensive. In the popular belief, charisma of a diplomat is essential, but in reality, such individuals in the diplomatic world are not too many. On the other hand, charisma may prove to be counterproductive when that diplomat's proposals or ideas are found to be non-implementable;

(e) A diplomat must be thoroughly professional to discuss the topic with his/her counterparts; and put forward his/her proposal to the counterparts clearly, in a simple language, and articulately. Where the issue or matter is required to be resolved on a multilateral basis, the diplomat must consider, in advance, what the counterparts might say and what kind of solution they might seek;

(f) A diplomat's knowledge must be multi-dimensional. Diplomacy is especially concerned with "the management of relationship between countries." The reason for this is that diplomacy is not solely concerned with international relations; it is instead a multi-disciplinary subject—management of relationship between and among countries;

(g) A diplomat must be a good negotiator. He/she must be prepared to listen to the other party/parties very attentively and must be prepared to consider the counterpart's ideas/proposals. Thus, he/she must be a good listener, patient, tolerant and unbiased; and

(h) Finally, a diplomat must be sagacious; he/she should be tactical, but must not tell lies. It is important to maintain his/her integrity and honesty in discussing issues with his/her counterparts. He/she must be careful that in discussing issues with the counterparts, he/she does not jeopardise the relationship between the two countries concerned, as by so doing he/she may also jeopardise the economic relationship between the two countries.

3.3 Interrelationship Between International Relations, International Law and Diplomacy

Experts in international relations seem to be convinced that there exists a close relationship between international relations and diplomacy. Indeed, a number of publications exist on the topic which have been written by experts in international relations.[4] Indeed, as discussed before, diplomacy has been defined by the Oxford English Dictionary as a skill of managing international relations, on the other hand, diplomacy may be defined as "the management of relationship between countries." The technique of management requires a thorough knowledge of developing and repairing, as the case may be, of relationship between States. But it may present a number of hindrances: (a) the other party's perception of national sovereignty; (b) the extent of inter-dependence between the two States concerned, whether for trade and mutual investment benefits; and (c) even for inter-State security reasons. But may all these issues be settled by political means only? Even though historically the relationship between two States has, in many cases, been very friendly, that relationship may break down for economic reasons or political or even from the perspective of religion. Take, for example, the relationship between Iran and the UK and the US. It has already been a long time that despite attempts made by both the sides and the intervention by the United Nations, the relationship between these countries remains strained. On the other hand, a rigid sense of sovereignty maintained even by a weak State may hinder developing inter-State relationship.

When however customary rules of international law exist, the power of making inter-State relationship becomes easier. Take, for example, the

[4] See, for example, F A Hartman, *The Relations of Nations*, New York, Macmillan (1962); see in particular Parts I, II and III.

right of innocent passage over the territorial waters of an enemy State. In the *SS Wimbledon Case*,[5] Germany refused to allow the Wimbledon, a British ship (carrying weapons) which simply sought innocent passage through the territorial waters of the Kiel Canal in Germany. Germany's argument was that grant of passage to the vessel would be contrary to the German neutrality regulations. When this issue was referred to the Permanent Court of International Justice by the British government, the Court maintained that Article 380 of the Treaty of Versailles laid down that the Kiel Canal must be maintained free and open to the vessels of commerce and war of all nations at peace with Germany. Furthermore, the German government had not at the material time, that is, when the Wimbledon incident took place, claimed any privilege to close the Canal to vessels of war of belligerent States at peace with Germany. Thus, the passage of a vessel carrying contraband of war through the Kiel Canal would not in any way affect Germany's neutrality.

Again, in the *River Oder Commission Case*,[6] Poland refused to surrender to the International Commission on River Oder on the grounds that a sovereign State is not obliged to surrender its sovereignty to an International River Commission in disregard of the fact that the management of each international canal and river in the world is governed by a River/Canal Commission, and each riparian State is obliged to implement their instruction for the maintenance of these waterways.

The Court maintained that one of the primary objectives of entrusting Commissions for the maintenance of all rivers and canals in the world is to create a "community of interest" in these waterways, and that this community of interest in these navigable waterways becomes the basis for a "common legal right," and such a right's basic feature would be to create perfect equality of all riparian States in the use of the entire course of the waterways, and that this forms the foundation of exclusion of any preferential privilege of any one riparian State in relation to the others. Thus, according to the Court, the jurisdiction of the International Commission of the Oder under the Treaty of Versailles (Article 331) extended to the tributaries of the Oder situated within the territorial jurisdiction of Poland.

[5] *Great Britain v Germany* PCIJ (1923) Series A, No 1.

[6] *Territorial Jurisdiction of the International Commission of the River Oder*, PCIJ (1929) Series A No 23.

These examples are sufficient to establish that sovereign States are required to maintain a flexible attitude towards their sovereignty when it comes to a "community of interests." Instead of fighting to establish which of the two disciplines, namely, Public International Law and International Relations, is better for diplomats to learn, it is suggested that they should have a minimum knowledge in certain principles of Public International Law and its Customary Rules which are binding for all sovereign States.

In the *Nuclear Test Cases*[7] between Australia, New Zealand (Fiji which eventually withdrew herself as a party to the dispute for her own reasons) and France, Australia and New Zealand alleged that France's acts in testing nuclear bombs in the sea for whatever purposes affected the sea to an immeasurable extent of damage to the sea environment. France, in reply, falsely invoked the principle of *res inter alios acta* (third parties are not to be held responsible for their acts under an international treaty) maintaining that by virtue of not being a party to the Nuclear Test Ban Treaty, France may not be held liable for testing nuclear bombs for non-warfare purposes. The International Court of Justice refused to accept France's argument on the grounds that the government of France may not be allowed to rely on the treaty principle of *res inter alios acta* as the Nuclear Test Ban Treaty established customary rule of international law from which no sovereign State, irrespective of whether a Party to the treaty or not, may not derogate from its provisions.

These are some of the reasons for suggesting that diplomats should be familiar with some of the principles of public international law which would also help them to settle inter-State disputes to which public international law rules would be applicable.

International relations might enlighten diplomats of the nature of inter-State disputes, but in most cases they are settled by an application of the relevant rules of public international law and/or bilateral negotiations.

Again, the Law of the Sea Convention, 1982, for example, has already developed customary rules of international law whereby while drilling on a Continental Shelf, no operator, whether their employer has accepted the Law of the Sea Convention or not, would be allowed to environmentally damage any part of the sea-bed, and if it does so, it will be held liable in financial damages.

[7] ICJ Reports (1974) at 253.

Diplomats should not ignore this issue, if his/her country is involved in this incident, and should be able to discuss it with his/her State lawyers. Thus, diplomats should possess basic knowledge in the important aspects of public international law, as they also should be familiar with the UN system, and obtain training in it, if necessary.[8]

3.4 On What Bases Should a Home State Select Its Diplomats?

At the initial stage diplomats may be reminded that until the Vienna Convention on Diplomatic Relations, 1961, and the Vienna Convention on Consular Relations, 1964, came into force, diplomats were mostly chosen on the basis of the selectors' own experiences in diplomacy and the family background of the candidate, which, in the contemporary period, may be regarded as an irrational procedure followed for the purpose. Diplomacy in the contemporary period, compared to that in the past, is very different as it has attained very complex dimensions in our time. The old-fashioned selection procedures must be reviewed. It is common knowledge that every State has some form of training system for diplomats, but it is felt that there should be a more advanced method of training embracing some of the important issues, namely, environmental, climate change, education in regard to the UN system, techniques of negotiating bilateral and multilateral treaties, private foreign investment agreements to name but a few. It is not for lawyers to do this work on their own, they should be guided by their diplomats; lawyers' main duty is to draft the agreements, contracts and so on, as the case may be. More importantly, over the two decades or so, a large number of inter-State warfares have taken place, indeed, some of them are still going on; diplomats should have expertise in war diplomacy in order to ensure that no wars and their attendant adverse effects take place. The Members of the United Nations through the UN Charter have undertaken the obligation not to resort to warfares or even the use of force. The best platform for a comprehensive discussion of this issue would be the United Nations, whether in New York or in Geneva. Diplomats should possess the knowledge of how the UN and its Specialised agencies work and how they may be of any assistance to them. It is a matter of shame that in the twenty-first

[8] See also G A Pigman *Contemporary Diplomacy: Representation and Communication in a Globalized World*, Cambridge, Polity (2010) at 17 et seq.

century the international community has failed on the issues of slave trade and slavery, drug trafficking, money laundering and cybercrime to name but a few. It is for diplomats to take up these issues with their governments, and adopt binding resolutions and work on it further for a successful implementation of that resolution with an international enforcement system operated by international enforcement officers along the lines of the UN Emergency Forces.

Trade diplomacy is another important form of diplomacy. Developing countries, in particular, have not performed as well on the WTO platform to protect their own interests, in terms of tariff negotiations and/or quota allocation for export trade of certain commodities in which many of the developing countries possess the expertise to satisfy the quality most of the developed countries look for.

Many government ministries are now required to review their practice as to the selection process(es) of diplomats, and their traditional attitude of keeping diplomats under their rigid instruction regimes without allowing them any reasonable degree of freedom but within the remits of the government's policy needs to be reconsidered too. A degree of dynamism particularly in respect of novel problems should be allowed to diplomats without penalising them. Take, for example, some of the very eminent diplomats such as Henry Kissinger or John Kenneth Galbraith, who had themselves added new dimensions to their job. This is not to suggest however that diplomats, in general, should have the licence to exceed their mandate which they received from their foreign office, or in whatever other name(s) they may be known, but on the other hand, they should be allowed, where necessary, to go beyond the bounds of their rigid mandate to work in the new circumstance with notification to their employers.

This degree of freedom may be necessary to debate issues on behalf of their countries at international fora, namely the World Trade Organization, World Health Organization, United Nations Development Programme, UN Conference on Trade and Development, International Labour Organisation and so on. After all, based on these debates whenever a treaty or convention or resolution would be signed by State diplomats, they are required to be ratified by their State legislature or even by the head of the State, unless of course, their federal constitution provides that these instruments would come into effect only upon signatures of their national diplomats, and in that event there should be a close discussion between the head of the delegates and the state's Foreign Office, prior to his/her signing the documents.

In choosing and selecting their diplomats, the home State authorities should ensure that each of them has good oratory skill, knowledge in how to negotiate an issue on behalf of his/her government, in addition to the other qualities that each of them should possess, and these have already been identified in the first part of this chapter.

All diplomats should have training in conciliation, a peaceful method of settling inter-State disputes, and this training should be provided by experts in the home State, as conciliation should receive a high priority by every State as a very effective method of settling inter-State disputes, bearing in mind that war begets war, which has been prohibited by the UN Charter, although unfortunately, as stated earlier that currently the world is torn with warfares. No foreign State should intervene in fuelling a state's enemy relationship with another country. States particularly those in the developing world should maintain the principle of equality between male and female diplomats; women, as human resources, should be developed to participate in responsible positions on behalf of their States. They should follow the pattern of appointments on an equal basis, whenever possible, like it is within the United Nations. There is no reason for not utilising women's services in developing countries in high positions. The education systems in developing countries should encourage women to go for university education and make it more cost-effective instead of adhering to the old-fashioned conservatism for keeping them as housewives and mothers only.

In fact, it is very important to remember that the UN declared the years 1975–1985 to be the Decade for Women; but how many States in the developing world, in particular, have implemented the message given to the international community?[9] Returning to the UN efforts made for gender equality, it would be appropriate to refer to some of the reports concluded by the UN or its subsidiary bodies. The UNDP Report of 2014 entitled *The Future We Want: Rights and Empowerment* provided inter alia that:

[9] See further UN, *The Convention on the Elimination of All Forms of Discrimination Against Women*, New York, The UN Treaty Collection (2017); see also J H Momsen, *Gender and Development*, London, Routledge (2004) at 14; UNDP, *The Future We Want: Rights and Empowerment: UNDP Gender Equality Strategy*, 2014–2017 at 3; UNDP, *Human Development Report 2016—Development for Everyone*, New York (2016) at 46; and M C Nussbaum, *Women and Human Development—The Capabilities Approach*, New York, Cambridge University Press (2000) at 106.

> Gender equality is not a "women's issue" but should concern and fully engage men as well as women. Equality between women and men is seen both as human rights issue and as a precondition for, and indicator of, sustainable people-centred development.[10]

The above statement made by the UNDP should be treated as an "eye opener." However, the UN action for the necessary forward steps for and development of women over the entire world was preceded by the international feminist movements which were initiated in the 1970s and indeed were followed up by the UN Decade for Women from 1975 to 1985. Coincidentally, the general level of public awareness for equality between men and women started growing in the Western world particularly since the 1970s, which, in fact, promoted an increasing presence of women in both commerce and political arena particularly in the Western world and within the world, mostly in the fields of education, health and corporate entities. The Gender and Development approach, commonly known as GAD, was developed in the 1980s; it actually originated in Britain; this concept viewed women as contributors to development—it also has a social dimension, and that has also been the primary theme of this work which supports rural development through indigenous people, including women. The caution should be entered that women in the Western world, whether in the cities or rural areas, have had more opportunities to educate themselves through televisions and radios, universities and further education institutions, but women in the developing world, living in the rural areas, have limited facilities or none at all in many areas. But for this reason the Western world should not undermine women in developing countries. Of course, in the urban areas in the developing countries women do have opportunities for higher education, but the higher costs of education may only be borne by the well-to-do families. There is little point, in the context of this work, to examine how the wide gap between women in the West and those in developing countries' rural areas may be narrowed down. As a starting point, however, capacity-building of women in the rural areas in developing countries has been recommended. Eventually, they will need higher education institutions, in the form of colleges of further education and universities in their areas.

[10] Op. cit., at 27; see also UN Agenda to end poverty by 2030, UNDP, *Human Development Report*, 2016, op. cit.

Home States should also ensure that diplomats are prejudice-free. They must not have any bias for or against a country and the peoples therein. Take, for example, mankind's own history—not only the Roman Empire's history which is full of warfares, but similar history became evident in most parts of Asia too. Colonialism tends to ignite hatred in many towards the colonial powers, but colonisation proved to be a historical phenomenon in the contemporary period of time. Thus, diplomats originating from former colonised countries, if and when posted in a former colonial power's jurisdiction, should not bear any prejudice against them. Indeed, many highly qualified people of non-white origins now hold very high positions not only at reputable academic institutions in the Western world, but they are also promoting ideas in other institutions too.

3.5 What Should a Diplomat Do When Posted in a Foreign Jurisdiction?

This issue should be considered from four points of view: (a) when a diplomat from a rich country may be posted in a poor country; (b) when a diplomat from a poor country may be posted in a rich jurisdiction; (c) when a diplomat from a rich country may be posted in another rich jurisdiction; and (d) when a diplomat from a poor country may be posted in another poor jurisdiction. Initially, it should be pointed out that in each of these situations, diplomats prior to their leaving for another jurisdiction should familiarise themselves with certain basic information on the foreign jurisdiction, namely, history, geography, the extent of human and natural resources, the current import-export situation between the two countries; the foreign jurisdiction's primary sources of income and the extent of their expenditures; which countries are treated to be the enemy countries by the foreign jurisdiction; an account of their internal problems, climatic conditions and so on, although their own Missions will also provide the basic information on the host State. However, if possible, such a diplomat should try to learn the host country's language prior to his/her departure for the foreign jurisdiction, although the English language is spoken by most of the jurisdictions in the world. There now follows a basic discussion of each of the options identified above.

3.5.1 When a Diplomat from a Rich Country May Be Posted in a Poor Country

Assume that the diplomat has had the basic training in diplomacy prior to his/her leaving for the receiving State, he/she will be required to satisfy the Protocol of the receiving State. He/she should also be familiar with the local custom as soon as possible so as to be able to greet them properly. Diplomats from rich countries posted in a poor country should not display by gesture or through expressions any prejudice against the poor country. The diplomats must be there to establish rapport in order to ensure that both the parties benefit economically, technologically or otherwise from that rapport. The primary objective of this kind of relationship would be to mutually gain from each other, namely, through import-export trade between themselves, and perhaps open up discussion of investments to be made by the developed country which would benefit both the parties. The ideal payment systems have been discussed in a separate chapter of this work.

It is re-iterated that it is so important for a diplomat to acquire as extensive knowledge as possible in order to ensure that the poor country may also offer benefits to a rich country particularly in the form of low industry products, textile and/or leather products or even agricultural products; and the kind of trade deal that would be possible for the rich country to make to the receiving State.[11]

Instead of borrowing money from the rich sending State, the poor receiving State should make attempts to open up new avenues to earn money with the help of the developed sending State. This may be achieved by applying the "buy-back" policy whereby no money will move from one jurisdiction to another. Under this system the foreign investor will be able to purchase very high-quality product at a very moderate price,[12] in addition to the indigenous people having the advantage of capacity-building. The representatives of the poor country (the receiving State) should not feel inferior to the diplomats from the sending State located in their country, and should seriously consider the economic dimensions to foreign policy-making, through their foreign office or in whatever other name they may be functioning. It must be emphasised that under no circumstances should either party do anything in consequence of which the negotiating process does not meet a "sudden death." This issue has received attention in a separate chapter of this work.

[11] The first part of the discussion is also equally relevant to the other sub-items too.

[12] See further S K Chatterjee, *Trade Finance*, London Routledge (2006).

3.5.2 When a Diplomat from a Poor Country May Be Posted in a Rich Country

As stated earlier the discussion in Sect. 3.5.1 is relevant to this section too.

When a diplomat from a poor country may be posted in a rich country, he/she should not suffer from any inferiority complex, and his/her primary duty should not be to arrange loans only; high debts for any country make her balance of payments position very adverse. His or her primary duty would be to put the rapport between the two countries on a firm footing.

The diplomat from a developing country while posted in a rich country should draw the attention of the appropriate authorities in the receiving State his/her country's potential and arrange mutual business opportunities, always with the prospects of building capacity for the country's human resources, which are often neglected by the developing countries, in general. The diplomat from the sending State should extend ideas of mutual cooperation rather than giving in to the demands of the rich receiving State.

The diplomat from the sending State during his/her office in the receiving State should open up all sorts of dialogues be they relate to business or education, including research projects which would provide the poor country's people technological knowledge in order to reach efficiency in the future. This kind of efforts would in due course minimise their dependency on rich countries.

3.5.3 When a Diplomat from a Rich Country May Be Posted in Another Rich Country

Once again, the first part of the discussion in Sect. 3.5.1 is relevant to this section too.

The horizon for business, education, research between rich countries is unlimited. Diplomats from two wealthy countries are supposed to know the potential each of them has; furthermore, they should also initiate discussion as to research and educational programmes between the two jurisdictions, in addition to joint technological and industrial programmes. It is doubtful whether rich countries would be interested in staying with their agricultural sectors as it will not be cost-effective for them to do so. This is precisely what is happening in the rich world, in general.

Rich countries' main assets are human resources, unless, of course, certain special industries such as pharmaceutical, hotel and entertainment, building, banking, shipping and insurance industries are also advanced. This is why it has been stated in the early part of this section that the horizon of business, education and so on in these countries is unlimited. Therefore, diplomats from two rich countries should engage themselves in joint programmes provided these programmes' structures do not run counter to the competition policy of either partner. These countries can jointly develop security programmes too.

Rather than lending funds to developing countries, it would be more creative of them to develop industries and human resources in those countries so that eventually they could join them for import-export trade, benefit from their high-quality products, manufactured with their scientific knowledge, and buy them at a reasonably low cost.

3.5.4 *When a Diplomat from a Poor Country May Be Posted in Another Poor Country*

Again, the first part of the discussion in Sect. 3.5.1 is relevant to this section too.

Contrary to the popular belief, constructive discussions between diplomats from two poor countries can be very useful and far-reaching. Here, both the parties are of equal standing, and it should be much easier for them to develop rapport between themselves.

They should identify their strengths and weaknesses first. They should not ignore their human and agricultural resources. In fact, they should develop their rural areas, including the people therein. Capacity-building of people may be done jointly with a competent rich country which has experience in providing training in capacity-building. They may together approach foreign corporate entities to set up branches in rural areas and provide capacity-building too. They can also arrange mutual trade between themselves, but not encourage migration of people between themselves by following an open-door policy.

In order to invite private foreign investors they may agree to develop or re-draft certain legislation, namely, foreign exchange, import-export trade, including restrictions on it, intellectual property law, environmental legislation, and also identify their exclusive jurisdiction. They must also develop a good banking and insurance system with good provisions for governance, but most of all, they should make their judiciary entirely separable and separate from their executive organ. In the event of their failing to do so, private foreign investors (transnational corporations) will be choosing to submit their investment disputes to arbitral tribunals of their choice, which alternative option developing countries should avoid. No developing country should enact any legislation which may not be effectively enforced by qualified enforcement officers. Diplomats belonging to developing countries should develop a joint security system between themselves, and where necessary jointly seek help from a relevant developed State.

3.6 Conclusions

The opportunities for two countries working together in their own interests are manifold, and yet they should be in touch with other countries, particularly, the developed countries in regard to their mutual interests as identified above. Diplomacy is not only about developing inter-State relationship, but also about other matters too, namely, settling inter-State disputes through negotiations and conciliations; to develop mutual security system, and mutually advantageous import-export trade system; to strengthen each other's knowledge in certain mutually agreed matters; to create opportunities and freedoms for all and, in particular, to recognise the role that women can play in the development process in a country, particularly in the rural communities; to mutually develop public awareness programmes and so on.

Diplomacy between two developed countries may be significantly different from that between two developing countries. But it is through the joint efforts of all countries, rich or poor alike, that certain contemporary problems, namely, drug trafficking, money laundering, cybercrimes, warfares, slavery and slave trade to name but a few may be effectively dealt with.

There is no reason why developing countries may not join the same platform along with the developed countries to deal with certain damaging problems which adversely affect both sets of countries, and should utilise the UN forum effectively in a united way rather than dwelling upon their weaknesses, bearing in mind that States are to a large extent responsible for their inefficiency, wherever identifiable, rather than remaining indifferent to them.

CHAPTER 4

Women's Role in Negotiating Diplomatic and Business Deals

4.1 Introduction

Women are a major source of human resources in all societies, and yet, almost the entire international community tends to ignore these resources perhaps mainly because of their age-old perception that women are supposed to look after their families. One should not blame only the societies in the developing countries on this issue, some of the rich countries are also trying to rectify this problem; they seem to be changing their attitude towards qualified and well-trained women in their societies by offering them high positions at universities, banks, insurance companies or large corporate entities. It is also worth noting that there is occurring a new phenomenon in the English parliament which is reflected in the significant number of female members in it, about 50–51%.

If one now thinks seriously of the views held by people, even in the twenty-first century, about women in many of the developing and developed countries it is bound to be very depressing indeed; the general understanding of women in such communities has been that in accordance with the societal practice, they should take care of their family, rear their children and sometimes help out their husbands, if they can. Thus women are also in a dilemma: whether they should stay back home to rear their family and look after their husbands or they should go out in the wider world to try to see what awaits them in their life.

C. Chatterjee, *Negotiating Techniques in Diplomacy and Business Contracts*, https://doi.org/10.1007/978-3-030-81732-9_4

On the other hand, it was from Great Britain, that during the two World Wars, many women joined the armed forces mainly as nurses, drivers, code-breakers and so on, which was a very good example of involving women in warfare-related work.

Female students started to join the British universities in large numbers mainly from the mid-1960s; by the same token, there were very few female academics as readers or professors in the early days, although since the 1980s there have been universities in Europe and in the UK including Oxford and Cambridge in which appointments of women are encouraged.

However, some Asian countries may challenge the above statement. For example, India takes pride in maintaining that Nalanda University is much older than the University of Oxford. Without going into any controversy on this issue, it may safely be maintained that until recently higher education for women in almost all countries failed to receive any priority by the governments concerned.

Thus, one should really ask oneself the simple question—why? The answer is simple too—prejudice against women; this prejudice has a very long history; therefore, people in the modern age conveniently fall back on that "prejudice." The United Nations took the initiative to change this societal attitude as means of eradicating this prejudice. It declared the years 1975–1985 to be the Decade for Women; unfortunately, the progress has been rather unsatisfactory. However, developmental organisations are currently engaged in promoting equality for women. But societies have to appreciate that discrimination against women simply leads to the loss of human resources.

At this point, one should identify the major effect of discrimination between men and women: women, in general, have fear of exploitation at work, forced marriages particularly in developing countries, domestic violence which is now a crime in England and Wales, discrimination in wages and/or salaries. There also exists a general bias in favour of men as to their characteristics: strength, masculinity, more rational than women, can be very charismatic too. On the other hand, women in general are perceived to be emotional, physically weak and requiring protection and often lacking confidence in themselves.[1]

[1] See further J A Tickner and L Sjoberg, "Feminism", in T Dune, M Kuani and S Smith (eds), *International Relations Theories—Discipline and Diversity* (latest edition), Oxford, Oxford University Press at 180.

As stated earlier that the assumed subservient position of women in societies is based on a very deep-seated prejudice against them. This prejudice portraits a woman as a mother and a caretaker of her children; they are generally perceived as naturally caring people. One should also realise why the nurses in almost all hospitals in the world are predominantly female. Usually in almost all countries the nursery and primary teachers are mainly women as this profession is often thought of as a caring one. This unfounded practice supported by most of the States belonging to the international community has already demoralised women in societies, in consequence of which a large quantity of human resources in almost all countries in the world remain unutilised.

In the Western world, the process of bringing in the necessary changes on this issue has been painfully slow. This discrimination between men and women is simply unjust. Legislation cannot treat prejudices in the minds of people; it is just like racial discrimination, which is often exercised covertly.

In this chapter an attempt is being made to examine the real effect of the changing approaches adopted particularly by various international fora.

4.2 A Critical Analysis of the Changing Approaches to the Gender Inequality Issue

In its report entitled *The Future We Want: Rights and Empowerment—UNDP Gender Equality Strategy 2014–2017*,[2] it stated, inter alia, that:

> Equality does not mean that women and men will become the same but that women's and men's rights, responsibilities and opportunities will not depend on whether they are born male or female. Gender equality implies that the interests, needs and priorities of both women and men are taken into consideration—recognising the diversity of different groups of women and men.[3]

The above statement is correct and unambiguous; however, it is a man-made policy not to allow women equal rights. The bases for this are totally

[2] UNDP, New York, 2014.
[3] Op. cit., at 27.

unfounded—prejudice, as has been stated before. In examining the UN Sustainable Development Goals, 2015,[4] its Goal No. 5 clearly stated that:

> Achieve gender equality and empower all women and girls.

At this point, it would be apposite to identify the events that may have contributed to a certain extent to changing the global attitudes towards women:

1. The UN Decade for Women from 1975 to 1985
2. The increasing presence of women in the political fora at an international level
3. The greater participation of women's organisations, mainly, in the form of non-governmental bodies, wherever possible[5]

Since the UN Decade for Women (1975–1985), the movement for equality of men and women has received recognition in almost all societies in the West, but unfortunately, that is not the position within the civil societies in the developing world. Women in the developing world need more education and facilities for education to raise the level of public awareness, which eventually should provide them with the sense of rights and freedoms together with a sense of duty towards their societies. This latter issue has attained urgency particularly in relation to the protection of the environment and climate change. Women can no longer be kept behind the curtains; they must be allowed out of their limited family circles.

Importantly, gender equality may not be achieved unless a high level of awareness is achieved in the communities of men. It is for men to appreciate that women have a significant role to play in societies, including the so-called high-powered employment. Inequality between men and women is worse than racial discrimination between the people of white and non-white complexions which in effect is based on prejudices. In the case of inequality between men and women both developed and developing countries are equally to be blamed. This is not to suggest that international movements through the truly international organisations and

[4] UN (2015) Resolution Adopted by the UNGA on 25 September 2015 (A/Res/70/1).

[5] See further D Thorburn, "Feminism Meets International Relations", 20 *SAIs Review*, No.2 pp. 3–4.

non-governmental institutions are of no use; on the contrary, they rightly highlight the urgent need for gender equality; but the evil still resides in our homes, and on this issue there hardly exists any differences between the perceptions of men in the Western world and those in the developing world; nevertheless, women in the developing world, in general, are not educationally as advanced as women in the developed world, other than those who reside in the urban areas. This is because there are no shortages of further and higher educational institutions in the urban areas in the developing world and it should not be forgotten that many highly educated women, political leaders and so on have been produced by a number of developing countries. Thus, it should be possible for developing countries to make women aware of their basic rights and freedoms, through education and training. Nothing is more shameful than when a country owing to the lack of policies and enforcement of those policies leaves human resources unexploited.

According to at least one author,[6] it would not be fair to criticise women in non-Western societies without possessing any thorough knowledge of those societies. But what are the principal differences between women, in general, in the Western world, and those, in general, in the developing world? The main difference would be primarily in regard to the women living in the rural areas in the developing world. They are not only the victims of the deep-seated prejudices but also they have very little or sometimes no opportunities to formally educate themselves to appreciate the importance of human freedoms and personal development.

Attention of the governments concerned should be drawn by the UN authorities on this issue for achieving change on the issue of gender equality over a reasonable period of time. Gender inequality is prevalent in the West, but unfortunately, it is very ingrained in the minds of men in the developing countries and forms part of their societal life.

Women in all societies in the world have been represented as an image of mother and wife, an embodiment of affection and care. This prejudice-based image of women entails a very long history; gradually, it formed a societal image throughout the world. That image is still prevalent in the Western world too. Women are known as people of fairer sex, kind and motherly, and they are supposed to show their sense of care to everybody.

[6] See further C T Mohanty, "Under Western Eyes, Feminism, Scholarship and Colonial Discourse", *Feminist Review*, vol. 30, No. 3, pp. 61–88.

This being the primary view of men about women, can any legislation change that view? It has therefore already been stated that men everywhere in the world need to change their perception in order to achieve the target of gender equality. In the UK, a degree of gender equality has become evident in high-ranking corporate positions, but that has been achieved owing to the pressures brought to bear upon them by various organisations, including non-governmental bodies.

Contemporary movement on gender equality has been very much concerned with the "empowerment" of women, but "empowerment" is the result of a process—what would that process entail bearing in mind that people are often slow in changing their attitudes towards women.

The issue of "gender equality" is not a one-sided problem—the factors which ought to be considered in this context are: how do men perceive women's position in societies, family life and in other spheres of life; secondly or conversely, to what extent women themselves would like to be empowered and relegate their traditional duties to their family and children? A balancing act would thus be necessary in order to resolve this problem.

In this context, this author wishes to make it clear that he is in full support of the idea of gender equality; hence he is raising the question whether both rich and poor countries thought about the means of eradicating the deep-seated prejudices held by men against women? On the other hand, what is the real view of the women's communities in the world on the issue of gender equality and the extent to which it should be promoted, bearing in mind that many women may not like a total empowerment as it might unduly disturb the family fibre, which is an important issue to maintain coherent societies. It is a difficult choice, but may be achieved if only prejudice is eradicated from the minds of both men and women. Empowerment only in one part or two of the world would be a "job done" partially. "Empowerment" seems to be a "domineering" term; everything may be achieved through understanding and effective negotiations between the two parties concerned. It is of utmost importance to provide education and training initially at primary and secondary levels in order to enable them to understand what empowerment stands for. Ordinary people in societies still seem to believe that attaining "empowerment" at the cost of integrated "family life" might be counterproductive particularly from the standpoint of the children's welfare, the future generation.

Empowerment's objectives are clear, but the methods of reaching those objectives may be quite difficult. A short list of the factors that have to be satisfied would be overcoming the deep-seated prejudice in the minds of both men and women, which may also be found in the minds of policy-makers. A holistic plan needs to be adopted at a State level first; those who are already advanced on this issue can also be referred to as examples of what may be achieved, and how they have achieved it.

4.3 A Critical Examination of the Hindrances to Gender Equality

The opening statement to the Convention entitled "Elimination of All Forms of Discrimination Against Women" (1979) is very significant:

> ... the full and complete development of a country, the welfare of the world and the cause of peace require the maximum participation of women on equal terms with men in all fields.

This Convention was adopted by the UN General Assembly and it entered into force as an international treaty on 3 September 1981. In reality, it was a document which was developed by the UN Commission on the Status of Women, a body established in 1946 with a view to monitoring the situation of women and to promote their rights. One of the objectives of this Convention is to explain the meaning of "equality" and how it may be achieved.

Prior to this Convention, the Convention on the Political Rights of Women was concluded in 1952; and Article 7 of the 1979 Convention incorporated the most important theme of that Convention, which has received attention in this chapter. Again, the basics of the Convention on the Nationality of Married Women, 1957, have been integrated under Article 9 of the 1979 Convention.

The Preamble to the 1979 Convention is rather long; therefore, in view of its importance to the understanding of the Convention in its entirety, a brief account of its philosophy is being given. In order to satisfy the justification for this Convention, it referred to the Universal Declaration of Human Rights which affirmed, inter alia, the principle of "... the inadmissibility of discrimination" and proclaimed that "... all human beings are born free and equal in dignity and rights and that everyone is entitled to all the rights and freedoms set forth therein, without distinction of any kind, including distinction based on sex."

After referring to the UN efforts to promote equality of rights of men and women through various conventions, resolutions and declarations, the drafters regretted that despite these efforts made by the UN, "... discrimination against women continues to exist." This is why it has been stated that the international institutions must first be actively engaged in eradicating the prejudices in men and women in all societies.

The drafters of this Convention registered their high ambition in regard to the main objectives of the Convention, by stating that

> Convinced that the full and complete development of a country, the welfare of the world and the cause of peace require the maximum participation of women on equal terms with men in all fields.

The thorny question remains, whether given the depth of prejudice prevailing in the world, society and in men against women and *vice versa*, the aspirations of the drafters may be soon fulfilled.

The real nature of the problems in attaining gender equality was indirectly identified by the drafters when in the Preamble to the Convention they stated that:

> Bearing in mind the great contribution of women to the welfare of the family and to the development of society, so far not fully recognized, the social significance of maternity and the role of both parents in the family and in the upbringing of children, and aware that the role of women in procreation should not be a basis for discrimination but that the upbringing of children requires a sharing of responsibility between men and women and society as a whole.

What the Preamble to the Convention has stated is correct, but the question remains given the nature of societies we currently live in, whether men and women will have the mentality and understanding that gender equality should be achieved as soon as possible.

The Bridging Platform for Action, which originated at the UN Conference on Women in 1995, emphasised the importance of developing the full potential of female children and hence an enabling environment should be allowed to be developed by governments in order to allow them to develop their spiritual, intellectual needs for survival, and of course, their equal rights (gender equality) must be safeguarded.[7]

It was again at Beijing that the issue of promoting the goals of gender equality in the interest of all humanity was strongly advocated; furthermore, with the end of the Beijing Conference, UNDP also publish on an annual basis *Human Development Report*[8] to highlight the cause of gender inequality, and hence the Gender Equality Strategy 2014–2017 was adopted. Without giving any more details of the UN activities on this issue, it may be maintained that "gender equality" has already made its mark in most parts of the world, but as stated earlier, the public authorities in the vast majority of States in the developing world are lagging behind owing to the reasons stated before.

Two decades ago, Martha Nussbaum, in her work entitled *Women and Human Development: The Capabilities Approach*[9] emphasised, with a view to empowering women, an approach which was also advanced by Amartya Sen[10]; it would simply mean two things: (a) that each person is worthy of respect, male or female; and (b) that women should also be provided with opportunities to increase their capabilities—the capacity-building approach. This should eventually raise their public awareness levels too.

In developing countries, there exist at least three inadequacies in policy-making: (a) that in general, the importance of human resources is neglected; (b) there hardly exist any concrete policies for their intellectual development primarily owing to the prejudices held by men against women—they should look after their families; and (c) they should not be outward-looking—the family circle is their circle.

"Empowerment" should allow women their freedoms and rights, but the dilemma is that the reality is different in most parts of the world. Would the public authorities in all parts of the developing world take the initiative to change the reality? Paragraph 2 of Article 28 is re-iterated on purpose to remind the reader of the provision of reservation made in the Convention on the Elimination of All Forms of Discrimination Against Women, 1979:

[7] See further *Bridging Declaration and Platform for Action*, 1995, Fourth World Conference on Women, UNGA Ref: A/CONF.177/20 (1995) and A/CONF.177/20/ADD. 1 (1995).

[8] See further UN *Supporting Gender Mainstreaming*, New York, the Office of the Special UN Adviser on *Gender Issues and Advancement of Women*, March (2001).

[9] New York, Cambridge University Press (2000).

[10] *Development as Freedom*, New York, Random House (1999) at 62–63.

> 2. A reservation incompatible with the object and purpose of the present Convention shall not be permitted.

This is the crux of the matter. The Convention, in effect, would not permit any Member State to enter any reservation to any of its provisions. But, a sovereign State may also rely on public morality or public policy of the country in order to avoid its obligations under the Convention even though it has ratified the Convention.

4.4 A Critical Analysis of Some of the Provisions of the Convention (CEDAW)

This Convention has been developed over 30 Articles and in VI Parts. Part I includes Articles 1–6. Article 1 defined the term "discrimination against women." According to this Convention, the above-mentioned term shall mean:

> ...any distinction, exclusion or restriction made on the basis of sex which has the effect or purpose of impairing or nullifying the recognition, enjoyment or exercise by women, irrespective of their marital status, on a basis of equality of men and women, of human rights and fundamental freedoms in the political, economic, social, cultural, civil or any other field.

Although the definition of the term "discrimination" appears to be broad, it is in conformity with the objectives of this Convention. But the fundamental question which has been raised before is that unless men's prejudices against women and *vice versa* are conquered, the prospects of achieving equality between the two genders will remain remote. Nevertheless, the international community's efforts and each government's efforts in both rich and poor countries will be a *sine qua non* for achieving this goal, which is worth pursuing.

Article 2 of the Convention has been solely addressed to the States that are parties to this Convention. The States are required, for example, to condemn discrimination against women in all its forms and agree to pursue by appropriate means, a policy aimed at eradicating discrimination against women, and to that end, undertake as many as eight specific obligations, namely,

I. To embody the principle of gender equality in the Member States' national constitutions or other appropriate legislation;
II. To adopt appropriate legislative and other measures, including sanctions, where appropriate prohibiting all discrimination against women;
III. To make provision for legal protection of the rights of women on an equal basis with men and to ensure that public authorities and institutions act in conformity with that provision;
IV. To ensure that everybody is refrained from committing any act of discrimination against women and that the same provisions apply to public authorities and institutions;
V. To take all appropriate measures to eliminate discrimination against women by any person, organization or enterprise;
VI. To take all measures, including legislation, and to modify or abolish existing laws, regulations, customs and practices which would constitute discrimination against women; and
VII. To repeal all national penal provisions which constitute discrimination against women.

Each of these provisions is very relevant and appropriate to the cause; however, the question remains whether States parties to the Convention would implement them when many of them, particularly in the developing world, are predominantly male-dominated societies. Hence, it has been mentioned before in this chapter that people of both genders need education on this issue; only legislation or prescriptive measures may not do. The important point to remember is that criminal law and the fear of prison sentences do not prevent criminals from committing crimes.

Articles 3 and 4 of the Convention do not provide any novel ideas, but re-iterate the Convention's primary objectives in a derived fashion. The latter part of Article 4 paragraph (2) mentions one of the problems of achieving gender equality. This provision states, inter alia, that:

> Adoption by States Parties of special measures … aimed at protecting maternity shall not be considered discriminatory.

Protection of the maternity right is an important right of women, and if this has to be maintained which ought to be maintained, then all the relevant parties, men, women and governments concerned are required to be enlightened, and that should be considered to be a serious first stage to achieve the objectives of the Convention.

The primary objective of Article 5 is to "modify the social and cultural patterns of conduct of men and women with a view to achieving the elimination of prejudices ... which are based on the idea of the inferiority or the superiority of either of the sexes or on stereotyped roles for men and women."

This is indeed the very theme of this chapter; it does not need any further comments. Paragraph (b) of Article 5 is an issue which men, in particular, should appreciate rather than standing in the way of gender equality. Article 5(b) states that:

> To ensure that family education includes a proper understanding of maternity as a social function and the recognition of the common responsibility of men and women in the upbringing and development of their children, it being understood that the interest of the children is the primordial consideration in all cases.

Article 6 requested the States parties to the Convention for legislative and other appropriate measures "to suppress all forms of traffic in women and exploitation of prostitution of women."

This Convention, for obvious reasons, aimed to be a comprehensive document; but with much hesitation it is stated that although the contents of Article 6 are relevant, given the nature of societies, in reality, would it be possible to achieve the objectives of Article 6?

Part II contains Articles 7–9. Article 7 presents an extremely relevant provision in regard to gender equality. It requests the States parties to this Convention to eliminate discrimination against women in the political and public life of the country, and to that effect, it requests the Member States to treat women on equal terms with men and allow women the right to:

(a) Vote in all elections including all publicly elected bodies;
(b) "Participate in the formulation of governmental policies, their implementation and to hold public office at all levels of government"; and
(c) Allow them to participate in non-governmental institutions concerned with public and political life of the country.

This is an unquestionably good provision; however, the fact remains that men and women, particularly in rural areas of developing countries, must be provided with opportunities to enter into the world of education with a view to raising the level of their awareness.[11]

By the same token, Article 8 of the Convention provided that the parties to this Convention shall take appropriate measures to ensure that men and women will have equal opportunities to represent their governments at an international level so that they can participate in the work of international organisations. Indeed, many highly qualified women even from developing countries hold high positions in the UN and its various offices. This also proves the point that if opportunities for higher education are offered to women, they should be able to compete with men for admission in their chosen programme of study/training.

Article 9 provides for an entirely new right for women. Paragraph (1) of this Article states that:

> States Parties shall grant women equal rights with men to acquire, change or retain their nationality. They shall ensure in particular that neither marriage to an alien nor change of nationality by the husband during marriage shall automatically change the nationality of the wife, render her stateless or force upon her the nationality of the husband.

Paragraph (2) of the same Article provides that:

> States Parties shall grant women equal rights with men with respect to the nationality of their children.

These provisions are very much based on the practice of the Western societies. It is doubtful whether the societies in the developing world may accept this practice.

Part III of the Convention has been developed over five Articles (10–14).

Article 10, in its entirety, has been devoted to one theme—educational opportunities for women on an equal basis with men. It is a rather long Article, but the basic summary of it would be that the States parties to this Convention shall take appropriate measures to eliminate discrimination against women so that they are entitled to equal rights to education, career development, access to higher education be it of a technical nature or

[11] See further W Easterly, "Democratic Accountability in Development: The Double Standards", 77 *Social Research*, No. 4 at 1076.

university education, access to the same curricula, the same examinations, same teaching by the same teachers, equal treatment in considering awards of scholarships or other forms of funds, adaptable and functional literacy programmes, the reduction of female drop-out rates, to facilitate admission to higher education programmes for those women who had to leave school prematurely, to allow them to participate in sports and physical education and other socio-family programmes on an equal basis with male students.

These provisions are also in a way addressed to universities and higher educational institutions, but in order to accommodate the principle of gender equality the accrediting bodies of the higher education institutions should also be prepared to show and apply leniency in regard to admissions of mature female and mature male students too, although universities in the UK, in general, have already made provisions for leniency towards mature students, both male and female.

The subject matter of Article 11 is Gender Equality in the field of employment. In addition to requesting the States parties to this Convention to implement Gender Equality by eliminating discrimination against women in the field of employment, it provides, in particular, the following: that the right to work is an inalienable right to all human beings; that the same criteria of employment should be applicable to both men and women—women must be allowed the right to freely choose their profession and employment; job security; the right to promotion; the right to receive vocational training and recurrent training with a view to keeping them up to date as to the new development that may have occurred in the area(s) of their employment; the right to equal remuneration including benefits for equal jobs; equal treatment in regard to periodic evaluation; their right to social security, sickness benefit, unemployment benefit; the right to protection of health and safety at the place of work, "including the safeguarding of the function of reproduction"; non-discrimination against women on the grounds of marriage or maternity; dismissal on the grounds of pregnancy or in regard to maternity leave; discrimination on the grounds of marital status; to allow women to continue family obligations with work responsibilities; participate in public life, and to "provide special protection to women during pregnancy in types of work proved to be harmful to them. The States parties to this Convention are required to review and revise their legislation, or other measures to protect the interests of women periodically." These provisions shall be reviewed periodically to consider inclusion of new provisions, if required.

Article 12 is concerned with healthcare of women on an equal basis with men; it provides for access to healthcare services for women too, "including those related to family planning." Paragraph (2) of the same Article provides that:

> States Parties shall ensure to women appropriate services in connection with pregnancy, confinement and the post-natal period granting free services where necessary, as well as adequate nutrition during pregnancy and lactation.

Article 13 aims at giving women equal rights with men in regard to "(a) the right to family benefits; (b) the right to bank loans, mortgages and other forms of financial credit; and (c) the right to participate in recreational activities, sport and all aspects of cultural life."

Article 14 of the Convention has been entirely devoted to the rights and benefits of rural women in recognition of the fact that they can also play significant roles in the economic survival of their families, pointing out however that States concerned should also take prompt action on this very important issue. It is a rather domestic issue, and if all States parties to this Convention take this issue seriously the situation should change. Article 14 hinted the idea quite clearly that currently women in the rural areas particularly in the developing world tend to work in the non-financial area, what the Convention described as "the non-monetized sectors of the economy."

It is important to summarise the contents of Article 14 which was developed over eight sub-paragraphs. As stated earlier that its principal aim is to achieve development for women in rural areas on an equal basis with men, although interestingly many men in the rural areas in a development process do not have much opportunities to develop their "capacity" either. According to this Article, women in rural areas shall be allowed by the authorities concerned to participate in "the elaboration and implementation of development planning at all levels"; to allow access to adequate healthcare facilities, including counselling and services in family planning; to ensure that they benefit from social security programmes (which are hardly available in developing countries); to allow them the opportunities to obtain all forms of training, education and whatever may increase their technical proficiency; to enable women to organise self-help groups, including co-operatives, in order to ensure that women will have equal access to economic opportunities in the form of employment or any other source of income; to allow them to participate in all community activities; in fact, this can be a source of another form of education through interaction with other people; to allow them access to agricultural credit and loans, appropriate technology and to participate in debates on land and agrarian reform; and finally, to enable them to enjoy good living conditions, including good sanitation, water supply and so on.

Part IV contains Articles 15 and 16. The primary theme of Article 15 is to "accord women equality with men before the law." To that effect the Drafters of this Convention requested the parties to the Convention to allow women, in civil matters, a legal capacity "identical to that of men and the same opportunities to exercise in that capacity." Thus women should have rights to conclude contracts of all nature and, if necessary, shall be eligible for all stages of procedure in courts and tribunals; by the same token, women should be treated equally with men in regard "to the law relating to the movement of persons and the freedom to choose their residence and domicile."[12]

Article 16 stated that in regard to marriage and family relations, the State parties to this Convention are required to eliminate discrimination against women, and in particular accord the same right to them about the following:

- The right to freely choose a spouse and to enter into marriage only on the basis of their free and full consent;
- The same right to enter into marriage;[13]
- No distinction between men and women as regards their rights and responsibilities during marriage and after dissolution; this is more important for looking after the children from their marriage until they attain the age of 18 or even thereafter;
- The equal right between men and women shall be allowed in determining the number and spacing of their children;
- The same rights and responsibilities to be recognised for women on an equal basis with men with regard to guardianship, wardship, trusteeship and adoption of children, but it is important to bear in mind that "in all cases the interests of the children shall be paramount;"[14]

[12] Article 15, paragraph (4).
[13] Article 16 (1)(a).
[14] Article 16 (1)(f).

- Husband and wife shall be allowed to exercise their personal rights at the same level, including women's right to choose a family name, a profession and an occupation;
- The same rights for both spouse shall be recognised in respect of the ownership, acquisition, management, administration, enjoyment and disposition of property, whether free of charge or for a valuable consideration;[15]
- The States parties to this Convention are required to "specify a minimum age for marriage and to make the registration of marriages in an official registry compulsory."[16]

Part V of the Convention has been developed over six Articles (Articles 17–22) of which Articles 17 and 18 are quite long. Each of these Articles relates to administrative and procedural matters:

- Article 17—Committee on the Elimination of Discrimination Against Women
- Article 18—National Reports
- Article 19—Rules of Procedure
- Article 20—Committee Meetings
- Article 21—Committee Reports
- Article 22—Role of Specialized Agencies

Finally, Part VI (the final part of the Convention) has been developed over eight Articles, and these have been categorised in the following way:

- Article 23—Effect on other Treaties
- Article 24—Commitment of States Parties
- Articles 25–30—Administration of the Convention

It would be appropriate to reproduce the entire text of Article 23 which has two sub-paragraphs (a) and (b).

Article 23

[15] Article 16, paragraph (h).

[16] Article 16, paragraph 2.

Nothing in the present Convention shall affect any provision that are more conducive to the achievement of equality between men and women which may be contained:

(a) In the legislation of a State Party; or
(b) In any other international convention, treaty or agreement in force for that State.

However, the reader's attention should be drawn to the following in respect of Article 28:

(a) That "a reservation incompatible with the object and purpose of the present Convention shall not be permitted."[17]
(b) "Reservations may be withdrawn at any time by notification to this effect addressed to the Secretary-General of the United Nations, who shall then inform all States thereof. Such notification shall take effect on the date on which it is received."[18]

Article 29, paragraph 2 provides that:

(c) "Each Party may at the time of signature or ratification of the present Convention or accession thereto declare that it does not consider itself bound by paragraph 1 of this Article. The other States Parties shall not be bound by that paragraph with respect to any State Party which has made such a reservation."

Article 29, paragraph 3 provides that:

(d) "Any State Party which has made a reservation in accordance with paragraph 2 of the Article may at any time withdraw that reservation by notification to the Secretary-General of the United Nations."
(e) Finally, according to Article 29 of the Convention, in case of any dispute arising between two or more parties in relation to the interpretation or application of the present Convention, attempts should be made first to settle that dispute by negotiation, and in the event of its not succeeding, then at the request of one of the disputants, it may be

[17] Article 28, paragraph (2).
[18] Article 28, paragraph (3).

submitted to arbitration. If however within six months from the date of the request for arbitration the parties become unable to agree to the composition of an arbitral tribunal, then one of the parties to the dispute may refer the dispute to the International Court of Justice.

4.5 Conclusions

The Convention on the Elimination of All Forms of Discrimination Against Women (CEDAW), 1979, was a laudable attempt made by the UN Commission on the Status of Women, in particular, to promote the Concept of Gender Equality in all societies of the world.

This chapter has already emphasised the importance of improving the capabilities of women (the Capabilities Approach) which should be a component of gender equality. Indeed, it ought to be stressed that during the UN Conference on Human Rights in 1993, the Vienna Declaration and Programme of Action was adopted by the UNDP and also followed the definition of "women's rights" provided by the Vienna Declaration[19] stated above. The UNDP and most of the non-governmental organisations in the world are very involved in promoting "empowerment of women" in all societies. But the hindrances to it have already received attention in this chapter.

"Empowerment of women" in its ordinary meaning stands for the techniques of giving powers to/or strengthening the position of women so that their voices are heard and that they do not feel ignored by the society they live in. Thus, the first agent to achieve this should be the local public authorities or the local leaders or even the male heads of rural families. Each of them should give encouragement to women as to their worth and how they could contribute to their own development process, and what women's self-confidence and leadership would stand for. If these sessions are held by locally qualified leaders, the local women may not be hesitant to raise any questions that they may have. This process should also take them through a useful learning process and feel encouraged to participate in such sessions—an effective learning process.

The UNDP's concept of women's empowerment would be more fitting for women in the Western world. Hence, the question arises is

[19] See UNDP, *The Future We Want: Rights and Empowerment—UNDP Gender Equality Strategy*, (2014) 2014–2017 at 27.

"gender equality" an essential component of "women's empowerment"? Whereas "women's empowerment" is principally concerned with providing self-confidence among women, particularly women belonging to families in the developing world, it also opens up opportunities for "capacity-building" through training and education which is a matter for the State concerned, and allowing them to seek high-powered employment in both public and private sectors and even seek political appointments. It is education that can satisfy each of these criteria. To a large extent, it is the lack of policy-making on the part of rural authorities and their governments that the measures for "empowerment of women" are not being adopted fully.

It is important to remember that women are, in general, vulnerable in societies, in the world. Only the degree of vulnerability varies from society to society; people should be aware of the fact that women in developing societies are more vulnerable than those in Western societies. Furthermore, the sources of vulnerability may also vary from society to society. Economic dependence of women on men in developing countries' societies combined with the lack of education makes them even more vulnerable to men. To this must be added the deep-seated prejudices on both sides, which affect women more than men. Bearing and rearing of children along with other domestic responsibilities keep women into the oblivion of the ethos of "gender equality."

Women in the rural areas in developing countries remain uneducated particularly owing to the lack of facilities and policies; thus, they take up very low-quality jobs to supplement the income of their husband, and children often follow the same route.[20] This is particularly the position of women, in general, in Africa, Asia and Latin America. However, the urban areas in the developing world are becoming developed in consequence of which within the same country, women of two types are created—one informed and educated, the other, not so informed and uneducated. Thus, a combination of factors in developing countries, particularly in rural areas, makes women very vulnerable.

As stated earlier, there exist certain insurmountable hurdles to overcome in order to enforce a system of education for women by the States parties to the Convention. The Convention provisions are generally being followed in certain States in the West. This has happened primarily because

[20] See further L Gezon, "Marriage, Kin and Compensation: A Socio-Political Ecology of Gender in Ankarana, Madagascar", 75 *Anthropological Quarterly*, No. 4 (2002) at 675–706.

of the pressures brought to bear upon the large industries and the financial world, such as the National Chambers of Commerce or organisations established for promoting businesses, in different names in different countries, or women's pressure groups in the UK, almost half of the members of Parliament in the House of Commons (the Lower House of Parliament) are women; however, the fact remains that there exist deep-seated prejudices in the minds of men against women and in consequence in the minds of women against men.

By contrast, the position of the States in the developing world, whether they are parties to the Convention or not, is entirely different, unless one refers to the position of women in the urban areas, in which many women are highly qualified, both professionally or otherwise, but are still treated, in general, as subordinate to men. This is predominantly owing to two reasons: (a) societal tradition and (b) deep-seated prejudices in the minds of men seem to have adversely affected the perception of the women as to their status in societies. They are also supposed to play their roles as wives and mothers. Traditionally, these societies have been male-dominated. The number of women holding high positions whether in the public or private sector is very limited; however, they deserve everybody's praise for their tenacity and high ambition which some of them have fulfilled. The position of women in the rural areas in the majority of the developing countries needs to be looked into seriously. It has been suggested in this chapter that their "public awareness" needs to be raised primarily through education unless any other viable alternative is found on this issue.

In the West, in general, the subservient position of women started changing primarily from the mid-twentieth century. Growing industrialisation combined with an increase in educational opportunities for women in the West contributed to overcoming the hindrances to gender equality in the majority of the States in the developed world. It must be hastened to add however that the level of deep-seated prejudices of men against women, in the West, is still remarkably high.

Over the past two decades or so, it has been a fashion for academics and non-governmental bodies, in particular, to write on Gender Equality, but the goal may not be achieved unless the deep-seated problems have been effectively dealt with. Trained women can be very good negotiators too.

CHAPTER 5

Negotiating Techniques in Import-Export Trade

5.1 Introduction

At the initial stage, it should be pointed out that from a legal standpoint it would be impractical to accept the term "international trade" because trade has always been bilateral, that is, between two parties in two different jurisdictions; it may at best be called "transnational trade" signifying that this type of trade takes place between two parties in two different jurisdictions. That is why, the simplest and yet the correct term for such trade should be import-export trade rather than the unsustainable popular term "international trade"; furthermore, the governing law of import-export trade contracts is hardly public international law, unless the two parties, be they governmental entities or even private parties, choose public international law as the governing law of their contracts; thus, in almost all cases, the governing law of transnational import-export contracts has been the law of one of the parties to the contract.

In the olden days, if, for example, an English person or a business entity almost invariably would strongly urge for English law as the governing law of the contract, simply because of either of the following reasons: (a) that an English party almost in most cases would be the seller, and in those days most of the merchandise used to be supplied by the seller; furthermore, import-export contracts usually used to be governed by the seller's law; and (b) that the English legal system and judiciary being outstandingly good, buyers did not oppose it, although it would be unfair to

C. Chatterjee, *Negotiating Techniques in Diplomacy and Business Contracts*, https://doi.org/10.1007/978-3-030-81732-9_5

maintain that there should be differences in status between the two parties to an import-export contract.

In this chapter an attempt is also made to identify the primary issues which should be negotiated and incorporated into an import-export contract, but the methods of payment or terms of trade do not really come under the purview of this chapter; thus a brief discussion of these has taken place in it. The caution should be entered that in negotiating the terms and conditions of an import-export contract, both the proposed buyer and seller should carefully examine the country profile of each country which may be obtained from the website of the World Bank; this document should allow a party to assess particularly the element of risks in doing trade with that country.

5.2 How Risks May Be Identified by Studying the Country Profile of a Country for the Purposes of Import-Export Trade

In studying risks, the party concerned should obtain the latest country profile of the country from the World Bank website, and in evaluating the risks, it must ensure that it does not proceed with any prejudiced mind either in favour or against that country. The following risks should be particularly studied in order to ascertain whether a buyer or seller would be suitable for doing import or export trade:

1. the market size and the approximate number of competitors already engaged in similar trade;
2. whether as an importing country it is subject to any import restrictions, or if an exporting country, whether its government has imposed any export restrictions on any product or services; some of the developed exporting countries may not be allowed to export, for example, leather or weapons, without the written permission of the governments of both the parties concerned;
3. the tax regimes in both the countries;
4. the climatic conditions and how often natural disasters have taken place in the near past;
5. the stability of the governments over the past decade or so;
6. in a developing country, the nature of foreign exchange regulations, as these regulations often restrict import and/or export trade;

7. incidence of expropriation or taking of property by the host government of the importing country, and the frequency thereof. Is it really a risk in the contemporary period?[1]
8. involvement of the countries concerned in warfares which may adversely affect import-export trade; and
9. the conditions of airports and seaports, and their loading and unloading systems, and durations of time needed for them.

5.3 Any Special Kind of Risk Associated with Public Bodies?

Public bodies in a State are usually bulk buyers; thus these institutions are able to attract large exporters; the latter often ignore the importance of studying risks against such prospective customers. The most they often do is to carry out what is usually known in the business world as "due diligence," without appreciating that no public body is obliged to disclose the true account of any information, let alone their burden of debts and bad relationship with certain governments. Due diligence process is usually carried out by a lawyer's firm in the local jurisdiction at a very high fee, but it proves to be a mere formality.

Like businesses with private entities, businesses with public bodies, not of all governments, can be risky too. One may not be able to attribute total honesty to anybody, public or private. Business with both types of entity may be risky. Here is the relevance of the doctrines of foreseen and foreseeable risks which the English courts seriously consider when one party to a contract seeks to enforce a *force majeure* clause in a commercial contract. The court concerned must establish "frustration" of the contract.

In the English judicial practice, four types of risks are considered: foreseen, unforeseen, foreseeable and unforeseeable. It is the unforeseeable risks which are considered to be the real risks for which a contract may be allowed to be rescinded; otherwise the foundation of a contract being in "good faith," courts may wish to adhere to this doctrine.

[1] See further C Chatterjee, "The Reality of Risks in Private Foreign Investment", *International Company and Commercial Law Review* (1996).

5.4 Negotiating Techniques in Import-Export Sales Contracts

This is a type of negotiating technique in which both the parties must aim at financial benefits for themselves. Whereas the seller must try to achieve the highest price for its product, the buyer's aim would be to buy the product at the lowest possible price. Apparently, it might sound like that the negotiating sessions take place between two enemies or opposable parties. But it is important to bear in mind that in this type of negotiating session, both parties are equal, and the parties should be allowed to proceed accordingly. In the business world, there is a saying "buy low, sell high," which, in reality, should not be the case.

However, in selling products, the seller must ensure that the products will meet the standards prescribed by the buyer's country by means of legislation or otherwise (the latter, by Codes of Conduct), and this issue is particularly important for sellers in a large number of developing countries. Hence, during the negotiation process, the buyer should make this issue clear to the seller, and if possible, by giving the seller specifications, in writing, or in the alternative, a copy of the relevant legislation or the Code. Over the past four decades or so, it has been the practice of many of the developed countries to buy products from the cheaper jurisdictions in the developing world. The developing world, in general, is able to do so by virtue of the materials being very cheap, and of course, due to the low level of labour costs. However, the manufacturing entities should ensure that a too low labour cost might accuse them of slave trade—thus, a balance on this issue has to be struck. Perhaps, there should be a system which would require sellers to confirm by documentary evidence whether they are promoting slave trade. The buyers should ask the suppliers to provide evidence that their workers are being paid reasonably good amount of wages which would be sufficient for their livelihood for the average families.

In selling the goods, the sellers should ensure that their goods will meet the standards set by the buyer's country. For example, in the UK, the Consumer Rights Act 2015 is in force, which would mean that the buyers may sell the imported goods to the consumers in the UK, only if these satisfy the legislative criteria. It is important to note that in the consumers' world the "buyer beware" rule—*caveat emptor*—no longer applies.

This is a relatively new phenomenon whereby the traditionally rich countries have started buying high-level products from the traditionally developing countries; this is indeed a praiseworthy improvement; some of the developing countries have been supplying products to Burberry or Gap; their efficiency level is now noticeably high. Thus, their sales become beneficial for both developed and developing countries.

Prior to their joining any real negotiating meeting, both the parties should, in addition to what has already been identified in the previous sub-sections of this chapter, also consider the following:

(a) whether the buyer, be it a developed or developing jurisdiction, when importing goods would be subject to any import or excise duty in the buyer's jurisdiction;
(b) guarantee in writing as to the quality of the product(s) and the duration of their life, where relevant;
(c) if a product is a multi-use one, those uses should be identified;
(d) the ingredients of the product;
(e) the country of make; and
(f) the circumstances in which the product should not be used.

5.5 The Topics Which Should Receive Attention of Both the Parties During the Final Negotiation Session

The preliminaries to this stage have already been discussed in the previous sections of this chapter. In this section, the final stage of negotiating import-export sales contracts and the important clauses which should be incorporated into such a contract have received attention.

5.5.1 The Contracting Parties

In this clause, the official titles of the parties, be they corporate entities or public entities, must be shown, with their addresses and company registration numbers in addition to the current addresses at which the headquarters of the corporate entities are located. In the case of a public entity the official title of the State, including its capital city, should be clearly shown on the contract. For example, in the case of Britain, the official title for business purposes is the United Kingdom; by the same token, the official title of America should be shown as the United States of America.

In the case of public entities, the name of the department/ministry, which is a party to the contract, should be clearly shown.

5.5.2 *The Goods*

Under this clause, the parties must clearly mention the goods which would be the subject matter of the contract. The full description of the goods, including their origin, purposes and their official name, should be clearly shown under this clause.

The weight, dimensions, colour, where relevant, of the goods should also be clearly shown. There are certain goods for which international specifications apply, namely, school and university desks and chairs (particularly their height and the gap between the chair and the desk); when these goods are to be the subject matter of the contract, it must be clearly mentioned that these goods must satisfy the international standards prescribed for them. The uses for which the goods will be obtained must also be clearly stated under the contract. In the case of perishable goods, the specific time by which the goods must arrive at the buyer's port must also be mentioned. But this clause is equally important for other goods also.

Automobiles and goods for industrial purposes must satisfy the requirements prescribed by the buyer's country; this condition also applies to most of the consumer goods, namely, textile or leather products meant for tropical or non-tropical countries; medicinal products manufactured in foreign jurisdiction must also satisfy the criteria, the language and specifications of the buyer's country. The parties should be clear about the description of the goods they will be dealing in; for example, in many countries there is no mention of differences between tables and desks; this clarification on goods to be bought and sold should be clear.

5.5.3 *Packaging*

By virtue of having very identifiable rules of packaging in England and Wales, this issue should not present many problems for the parties to decide on once they have agreed to the other terms of their contract. Of course, this issue has to be considered by the shippers as they are also governed by very stringent rules. It is important for developing countries to follow uniform rules also on this issue. Where however, for example, 10 items of each product should be in a package and therefore 100 items altogether in ten packages, but if the packages are made up of different number of products in each bag although the total number of packages is ten, the buyer will have the right to reject them as the packages do not conform to the order (ten in each package was a term of the contract).

5.5.4 *Delivery*

This is an important clause to incorporate into an import-export contract. Both the date of delivery and the port of delivery must be mutually agreed upon by the parties concerned. But the parties should also enter provisions for uncertainties, such as warfares which might require diversion of the vessels which in turn would take a longer time of journey than the usual. In the event of the diversion being unnecessary, the buyer can claim damages for the financial losses it might incur for the delay; this latter issue should be entered into the contract.

5.5.5 *The Price*

The determination of the price is a tricky issue; in preparing the invoice to be drawn on the buyer, the seller is required to bear in mind its cost price for obtaining or producing or manufacturing, as the case may be, the product, the transportation costs, port fees, loading and unloading charges and a transportation cost for carrying the goods from the port to the place of business. The seller should submit to the buyer a detailed breakdown of how he/it reached the price and the total costs to the prospective buyer. On the other hand, in the event of the buyer arranging its/his own transportation by road or by whichever other ways, the seller should exclude transportation costs.

The buyer and seller, who are public bodies, might opt for countertrade—goods against goods system. There exist various forms of countertrade.[2] This form of payment has a long history, and many traders still seem to suffer from prejudices against this form of payment. But it is quite prevalent in a number of countries. Furthermore, this form of payment helps save the foreign exchange reserves of the countries concerned. The international business community should consider this form of payment seriously. Incidentally, the government of the UK is very much involved in goods-against-goods form of trade with other countries.

[2] See further C Chatterjee, *Legal Aspects of Trade Finance*, London, Routledge (2006).

5.6 Terms of Trade

Over the years the international community has developed a number of trade terms of which the most popular ones are fob (free on board), cif (costs, insurance and freight), c f & i (costs, freight and insurance) and c & f (costs and freight). Of these terms, the most popular ones are fob and cif. Historically, fob is the oldest form of trade term as under this term the foreign trader (the buyer) would arrive in his/its boat at the seller's port, and put the goods on board free of charge. Once the goods have crossed past the ship's rail, the seller's risk is over.[3] When the fob term was devised, the concept of insurance did not exist.

In Britain, Edward Lloyd developed the concept of insurance. Cif term provided security against losses—the effect of the insurance policy to compensate any losses that might occur in relation to the consignment of goods. The costs of the insurance policy are usually borne by the buyer.

C & f is rather a risky term unless the buyer arranges his/its insurance policy.

C f & i has become rather popular over the past few decades. In this form of trade, usually the buyers in the receiving countries arrange their own insurance policy. Indeed, in quite a number of developing countries one can find a number of insurance companies which provide insurance policies, and the buyers in developing countries find it profitable to arrange their own insurance policy when they buy goods from the foreign sellers.

In addition to sending emergency medicinal products by air, there are certain other products which are not found to be suitable for journeys by boat, for example, silk and silk products.

5.7 Payments Through Banks

The traditional payment system through a bank in the buyer's jurisdiction has been for the buyer to open a letter of credit, which means the bank agrees to lend (credit) the buyer the amount of funds that the buyer would require to purchase the goods. After the goods arrive at the buyer's nominated port, and upon delivery of the goods and upon sale of the goods, the bank will have to be paid first with interest on the loan, as the bank will have a lien on the goods.

[3] See further Schmitthoff's *The Law and Practice of International Trade*, edited by C Murray, D Holloway et al. (eds), London, Sweet & Maxwell (latest edition).

In the unfortunate event of the goods on board being damaged or the ship sank causing all sorts of claims, the buyer will be able to recover his/its losses from the insurance policy.

The most reliable document on documentary credits is published by the International Chamber of Commerce in Paris with which all parties concerned should be familiar rather than leaving import-export trade-related problems to their lawyers.

Having pointed out certain risks embedded in import-export trade, even in regard to the transmission of funds to the seller's bank, it should be observed that this form of transfer of money from one jurisdiction to another still appears to be the safest method of payment by foreign buyers. It is also for the transmitting bank to take all precautionary measures to ensure that no money laundering activities come into a transaction process.

5.8 Settlement of Disputes

The governing law of an import-export contract has remained a thorny issue. As stated earlier that in the olden days there was a practice to incorporate English law as the governing law of these contracts in order to ensure that the disputes arising under these contracts should be referred to the English courts, without paying attention to location of the performance of the contract. It still remains uncertain whether the seller's place or the buyer's place is the place of performance. The EU believes that a seller's place may also be regarded as the place of performance. However, in reality, English buyers will be hesitant to accept that primarily because they do not have sufficient faith in the foreign courts. True it is that the English judiciary takes pride in its being the best judiciary in the world as it is totally separable and separate from the executive organ of the government which happens to be its appointing authority. Should however a seller voluntarily accepts the English jurisdiction for settling disputes that may arise under such contracts, then no problem may be foreseen.

If the above option does not work, then the following options may be tried: (a) negotiation, (b) conciliation and (c) arbitration. Of these three options, arbitration may present two types of difficulty: (i) contrary to the popular belief, it is quite a costly method of settling a commercial dispute; and (ii) the problems associated with the enforcement of the award in a foreign jurisdiction (in this context, the seller's jurisdiction) especially when both the parties have agreed that their arbitration would be governed by the New York Convention on Foreign Arbitral Awards.[4] The award-debtor's judicial authorities may decline to refuse an enforcement of the Award on the grounds that the enforcement of it would run counter to public policy or morality of the award-debtor's jurisdiction.

In view of the above, it is strongly recommended that in the event of a dispute arising under an import-export contract, the parties should make their best efforts to negotiate between themselves to settle it. Incidentally, most of the disputes (which is a very legal term) are, in reality, differences of opinion on issues between the parties; thus, they should really try to conciliate their disputes/differences in the presence of a qualified conciliator, whether in the buyer's or seller's jurisdiction, and settle their disputes/differences in a friendly fashion, which would also cost them much less than any other method of settling disputes/differences.

5.9 Conclusions

Trade pattern of most of the countries in the world, both developed and developing countries, has been significantly changing over the last three decades or so. The majority of the countries that have been traditionally regarded as "developing" are now quite competent in their agricultural and cottage industry sectors. Many of them are capable of manufacturing light industrial products, fine textile and leather products, in addition to developing IT, engineering and medicinal products. These products are usually supplied to the rich countries. Some of these countries are now exporting textile products for reputable fashion houses in the West. By virtue of the labour and material costs being quite low, the fashion houses and even some of the reputable departmental shops in the West have been purchasing products manufactured in many of the developing countries.

Many of the developing countries have been supplying agricultural and textile products, in particular, to developed markets, as the latter find them cheaper to buy than their own products, primarily because the wage level in the Western countries, in general, is quite high. Hence a shift in the marketing and sales patterns in these two sets of countries has become very manifest. In fact, from a political standpoint, this new pattern

[4] See further C Chatterjee, "Recognition and Enforcement of Arbitral Awards: How Effective is Article V of the New York Convention of 1958?" *International In-house Counsel Journal*, vol. 9, No. 36 (2016).

developed through transnational trade should form a new type of friendship between the countries in these two parts of the world.

In this context, one should also consider how the position of the developing countries, in general, may be strengthened in the world economy. It is not by aid from various institutions and States that may help develop these countries, and if that were so, then the developing countries should have been developed by now. Financial aid and borrowings simply accumulate debts for a country, and that is exactly what has happened to the developing world.

Transnational trade is a factor of development, but how may the net of this type of trade be spread? It is suggested that the current practice of negotiating private investment contracts needs to be reviewed urgently, and how may they be changed has been suggested in Chap. 3 of this book.

In so far as import-export trade is concerned, in negotiating these contracts the developing countries' buyers or sellers should try to negotiate new terms of payments, and where possible, take out insurance policies from home companies (on a c f & i basis); this should save money also for the buyer or seller as the case may be.

There is no harm for the buyer/seller belonging to a developing country to do trade on the basis of goods against goods, although currently it is confined to public bodies (in the form of countertrade or barter). This is suggested because many of the developing countries are now capable of manufacturing products to the standards specified by buyers of developed or even another developing country. This system of import-export trade should be liked by the central bank of the country as it will save its hard currency reserves.

Import-export trade offers opportunities to businesses to further their skills and knowledge; therefore, it may be suggested that on the basis of an import-export contract, the host may like to arrange capacity-building training sessions in order to ensure that as from the next order they become even more competent to manufacture the products to comply with the standards of the buyers. This is an important issue, because if the products of the developing countries are regarded by the Western world as of inferior quality then in course of time, the developing countries will stand a good chance of losing their business in the Western world. It is also important for them to know the extent of expectation and the nature of rights consumers have at least in England and Wales. It is particularly for providing protection to consumers that the Consumer Rights Act, 2015, was enacted in England.

CHAPTER 6

Negotiating Techniques in Ending Armed Conflicts

6.1 Introduction

In writing this chapter it would be most appropriate to remind the reader what the Members of the United Nations undertook to follow in order to maintain peace and security of the world. It is also important to remember that the United Nations was set up recalling the miseries that the two devastating World Wars brought to the mankind. It is also worth remembering that the constitution of each humanitarian institution must contain a philosophy which would be the driving force to perform the objectives of it and that its members must also abide by them and cooperate with the objectives of the institution.

The Preamble to the UN Charter States, inter alia, that:

> WE THE PEOPLES OF THE UNITED NATIONS DETERMINED
> to save succeeding generations from the scourge of war, which twice in our lifetime has brought untold sorrow to mankind, and
>
> to reaffirm faith in fundamental human rights, in the dignity and worth of the human person, in the equal rights of men and women and of nations large and small…
>
> AND FOR THESE ENDS
>
> to practise tolerance and live together in peace with one another as good neighbours, and

C. Chatterjee, *Negotiating Techniques in Diplomacy and Business Contracts*, https://doi.org/10.1007/978-3-030-81732-9_6

> to ensure, by the acceptance of principles and the institution of methods, that armed forces shall not be used, save in the common interest...

Article 1 of the UN Charter states the Purposes of it. Paragraph 1 of the said Article provides that:

> To maintain international peace and security, and to that end: to take effective collective measures for the prevention and removal of threats to the peace, and for the suppression of acts of aggression or other breaches of the peace, and to bring about by peaceful means, and in conformity with the principles of justice and international law, adjustment settlement of international disputes or situations which might lead to a breach of the peace.

Paragraph 2 of Article 1 provides that:

> To develop friendly relations among nations based on respect for the principle of equal rights and self-determination of peoples, and to take other appropriate measures to strengthen universal peace.

Paragraph 2 of Article 2 (which details the Principles on which UN is based) provides that:

> All Members, in order to ensure to all of them the rights and benefits from membership, shall fulfil in good faith the obligations assumed by them in accordance with the present Charter.

Paragraph 3 of the same Article provides that:

> All Members shall settle their international disputes by peaceful means in such a manner that international peace and security, and justice are not endangered.

Most importantly, paragraph 4 of Article 2 provides that:

> All Members shall refrain in their international relations from the threat or use of force against the territorial integrity or political independence of any State, or in any other manner inconsistent with the Purposes of the United Nations.

Each of the Principles laid down by Article 2 of the UN Charter is binding on each of the Members of the United Nations, although it is not clear how the UN may ensure that the states which are not members of the Organisation will act in accordance with the Principles necessary for the maintenance of international peace and security. But, by coincidence none of the non-members of the UN happens to be a powerful military State.

The UN Charter has also provided for its integrity by providing in paragraph 7 of Article 2 the following:

> Nothing contained in the present Charter shall authorize the United Nations to intervene in matters which are essentially within the domestic jurisdiction of any State or shall require the Members to submit such matters to settlement under the present Charter; but this Principle shall not prejudice the application of enforcement measures under Chapter VII.

It is not clear how should a Member State decide whether a matter is essentially within the domestic jurisdiction of a State,[1] particularly when the attitude of the international community is changing as to what should be considered to be a matter of "international concern." But when the Charter of the United Nations was drafted, the attitudes of the countries that participated in the Second World War, be they colonial powers, colonies or otherwise, were very determined to bring peace in the world.

Article 6 of the UN Charter states that:

> A Member of the United Nations which has persistently violated the Principles contained in the present Charter may be expelled from the Organization by the General Assembly upon the recommendation of the Security Council.

But despite misconduct on the part of many of the Member States of the United Nations, the UN has not expelled any of its Member States, as any expulsion of any of the Member States would amount to granting a licence to do anything it likes, and the UN would be unable to take any action, if necessary, against that State.

Many believe that the UN is a useless organisation, but the question remains who have made it useless, if at all? The answer is obvious. In violation of their undertakings at the time of accepting the membership of the UN, quite a number of States have either initiated or got themselves involved in warfares, which have already caused untold miseries not only to the victims of those warfares but also to the entire world. The number

[1] See further R Higgins, "The Concept of Domestic Jurisdiction in United Nations Practice" in *The Development of International Law through the Political Organs of the United Nations*, Oxford, Oxford University Press (1963); see Part II of the work, pp. 58–130.

of refugees is currently rising, and so are poverty in societies and death toll. Should the UN be blamed for all these irreparable damages to economies and untold miseries to so many people?

Genocide or a smaller version of it in Afghanistan, Haiti, Rwanda, Syria and Yemen to name but a few and its consequential adverse effects on those societies are being constantly ignored by the offending States. Thus, a number of the Member States are in breach of the obligations they undertook at the time of their becoming the members of the United Nations.

But it is interesting to note that none of the aggressor States nor the aggressed States have taken any action to negotiate to determine the cause of aggression and thereafter to resolve them. Article 33(1) of the UN Charter provides that:

> The parties to any dispute, the continuance of which is likely to endanger the maintenance of international peace and security, shall, first of all, seek a solution by negotiation, enquiry, mediation, conciliation, arbitration, judicial settlement, resort to regional agencies or arrangements, or other peaceful means of their own choice.

Paragraph 2 of Article 33 provides that:

> The Security Council shall, when it deems necessary, call upon the parties to settle their dispute by such means.

Furthermore, Article 37(1) of the Charter provides that:

> Should the parties to a dispute of the nature referred to in Article 33 fail to settle it by the means indicated in the Article, they shall refer it to the Security Council.

But how many aggressors or aggressed have referred their disputes to the Security Council or exhausted Article 33 or Article 37 provisions for that matter?

6.2 The Probable Causes of Warfares/Conflicts

It has been stated earlier that the primary cause of warfares is prejudice, usually based on race, religion, colour and so on. Prejudice does not admit of any reason. Prejudice-based warfares can happen between two parties following the same religion, such as that between Syria and Turkey. The war between the US and Viet-Cong was a war to fight off the spread of Communism, another kind of prejudice against another political-ism. Again, the Europeans sharing the same religion fought between themselves based on prejudices, that is, in the belief that one party is superior to the other.

Acquisition of land area by force has also been a factor of warfares at least in the past, especially when no correct demarcation of land boundaries existed. Hitler's war against the Jews, in fact, to eradicate the entire race, was nothing but a war of prejudices against the Jews.

After the Second World War, however, particularly after the statehood of the newly born countries, internal conflicts have become a common phenomenon within the developing countries to overthrow the ruling regime, primarily on the grounds that the regimes fail to grant any freedoms and rights to their peoples. Furthermore, such conflicts are also arising between races living within the same State.

These internal political disturbances, which are described by many authors as "conflicts," are mainly initiated by their leaders who want to be martyrs or even terrorists.[2] One should not be surprised if foreign parties also join them to provide support financially or even by supplying weapons. According to Paul Collier, such civil wars are more likely to occur in poor countries, with prolonged deteriorating economy, but more dependent on primary commodities, which, in fact, is a typical symptom of a poor economy.[3] On the other hand, some of the internal conflicts are based on prejudices against people of certain origins living in the country; these conflicts are usually prolonged—the country of their origin would not allow them to stay in there; if they seek refuge in a neighbouring country they will experience difficulties in staying in the second country. One of the recent examples would be the Rohingya Bengalis from Bangladesh; they sought refuge in Myanmar, a neighbouring country with Muslim population too. In the final analysis, the reason behind the rejection of Rohingya Muslims was simply prejudice—that they are not the Muslims of the kind Bangladesh would accommodate.

[2] J W Burton, "Peace Begins at Home—International Conflict: A Domestic Responsibility", 6 *International Journal of Peace Studies*, No.1 at 5.

[3] P Collier, *The Bottom Billion: Why the Poorest Countries are Failing and What can be Done About It*, Oxford, Oxford University Press (2008) at 34–35.

Internal conflicts became a common phenomenon during the colonial period. Although Indonesia gained her independence from the Dutch and became the first de-colonised country in the world, India, as the largest colony of the British Empire, had gone through internal conflicts, which ended up in bloodshed and deaths of innumerable, in addition to giving rise to a further division of India—a new country, Pakistan, was created. Ironically, Pakistan became independent one day before India attained her independence (on 15 August 1947). Internal conflicts mobilise student opinions for freedom and independence; they also give rise to terrorism and the rise of various political leaders to provide even more fuel to the independence movement. These internal conflicts also determine, rightly or wrongly, future leaders for the country concerned.

These internal conflicts may be confined to the territorial boundaries of the country concerned, but they can eventually turn into trans-boundary conflicts involving a number of foreign countries in it—all in breach of the relevant provisions in the Charter of the United Nations. Certain examples of the above-mentioned type of conflicts would be Afghanistan, the Congo, Iraq, Myanmar, Syria, Turkey and Yemen, to name but a few. Each of these conflicts attracted foreign powers, military weapons and even foreign army sent by the US and the Russian governments to Afghanistan.

The pertinent question to raise is what made the countries involved in full-fledged warfares to disregard the Geneva Convention, one of the principal aims of which is to protect civilians and to regulate the conduct of wars. This is precisely what has been indicated in the first part of this chapter. What is urgently to be achieved by the international community is to develop a strategy of conflict prevention, which is really a task to be performed by the Foreign Affairs offices of various countries and their high-ranking diplomats—this is where a very sophisticated form of negotiation is essential.

It is believed that apart from prejudice, the other reason for internal conflicts would be the dictatorial attitude of the head or leader of the State, who denies the fundamental rights and freedoms of people within the State, and the State judiciary will be totally under the control of the head or leader of the country. These heads or leaders of States do not trust their people, and believe in their total domination of them, even though the individuals' aspirations, in general, have changed. Effectively, these regimes can be described as the second form of colonisation. Many members of the United Nations seem to have decided to disregard the UN Charter provisions which they accepted at the time of their becoming the members of the organisation. This is precisely the reason why the basic and very relevant provisions of the Charter of the United Nations have been quoted at the beginning of this chapter.

From an academic standpoint, it may be stated that the heads or leaders of States seem to fit what Thomas Hobbes said in his Leviathan that people are opportunists and distrustful, they are power-mongers. The pyramidical structure of governments is very common within the developing world in disregard of the fact that the people, in general, in the developing world aspire to enjoy their rights and freedoms, which the people in the developed world enjoy.

Even many corporate entities in the Western world are now required to democratise the governance system within their large corporations whereby employees' participation in the governance of the corporation to which they belong becomes compulsory.

The dictatorial governments certainly contribute to internal conflicts, but nevertheless, diplomats negotiating these conflicts should clearly identify the real root causes of these conflicts and the extent of human sufferings which have impacted their economies should also be ascertained in order to be able to emphasise that during a negotiation process. It must be emphasised during a negotiation process that miseries are self-induced. It also ought to be re-emphasised that most of these internal conflicts are rooted in prejudices; thus the rulers have to learn how to overcome prejudices against people of other origins, religions and so on. Such atrocities require assistance, financial and military, from foreign countries, which unnecessarily complicates the situation and owing to the expenses involved in quelling the conflicts, which in almost all cases have failed, makes the country financially poorer and poverty deepens further.

Pure democracy does not seem to exist in any country; in fact, given the changing nature of the political firmament in every country, the entire precept of an ideal democracy may not be successfully established, and yet, there is no reason why non-dictatorial governance systems may not be established. A degree of liberalism may easily be operated, whereby both the people and the leader of the government will benefit.[4] This should also

[4] See further Immanuel Kant, *Kant's Principles of Politics: Including His Essay on Perpetual Peace* (1991), Translated by W Hastie, Massachusetts, Kessinger Publishing (2010); see also J Burton, op. cit.

be a point for the negotiating team—peace should be the normal State of life, not warfares.

The primary objective of democratisation is to build social cohesion among people of different origins and religious beliefs—the days of one-nation one State are over; we have to learn how to live in multi-cultural and multi-racial societies—leaders of countries, particularly in the developing parts of the world, need to appreciate this phenomenon. If one does an empirical study on this issue, one should be able to reach this decision too, otherwise conflicts in States with their consequential adverse effect will remain with us as a permanent phenomenon. Would any sensible individual wish to return to the internal conflicts to which, for example, the following countries became victims—Angola (1991), Bosnia (1995), Cambodia (1991), Croatia (1995), East Timor (1999), El Salvador (1991), Guatemala (1997), Kosovo (1991), Rwanda (1993) and Sierra Leone (1999)?

In fact, none of these conflicts should have occurred if only the leaders of these countries started democratising their societies and implemented legislation to that effect, but unfortunately, that did not happen in any of these countries. Thus, the cause of internal conflicts may only be attributed to the leaders' policies in the above-mentioned countries. Furthermore, the leaders of each of these countries totally disregarded the important UN Convention entitled The Convention on the Prevention and Punishment of the Crime of Genocide, 1948. Another important point to bear in mind is the probable outcome of sending external missions in settling internal conflicts, as in most of the cases listed above, the external missions failed to settle this type of conflicts. Conflict resolution should be carried out by the parties concerned with an intention to resolve them. When a conflict is entirely "internal" in nature, it is for the leaders of each group of people to participate to reach a resolution for the problems, perhaps in the presence of a qualified conciliator who would be extremely familiar with the causes of the conflict.

It has already been explained in this chapter that racial hatred, based on prejudices of the indigenous and external people, also has often been one of the causes of these conflicts; thus, it falls on the parties to come to their senses and try to narrow down the differences between themselves. No two foreign countries are involved in such conflicts; these are entirely localised and indigenous conflicts; it is for the hostile groups to iron out their differences. It is re-iterated that the presence of a third party who should be familiar with the root causes of the dispute/conflict only to regulate the discussion, and perhaps offer certain suggestions to the parties, reminding them of the adverse effect of continuing with their dispute/conflict, may be welcome.

6.3 The Conflict Resolution Tactics

Internal conflicts in countries are not a rural phenomenon—they have been with us for a very very long time indeed, and they are known to the informed people. If one remembers that most of the conflicts, if not all, are rooted in prejudice, which has no logical foundations at all. Internal conflicts emanate from internal causes; that is why, such conflicts should be settled by the leaders of the two parties which are the causes of conflicts.

As to the "tactics" neither party should give vent to anger; they should bear in mind that racial prejudice has no real legal foundation. The leaders representing the factions must appreciate that no historical example will do. Conflicts/disputes must be based on facts, not fictions or prejudices. This issue became quite clear in the Rwandan conflict, which actually led to an unforgivable genocide.

As background information, it should be stated that Rwanda has been torn with the internal conflict between the two factions: the Hutu and the Tutsi. In this conflict, the Hutus killed at least one million Tutsis in which then the Rwandan army and civilian population also joined. The State also extended its help to the conflict, and of course the media also contributed to intensify the conflict by inviting the population to participate in violent activities. In this context, a brief historical growth and development of Rwanda would be useful to add. Rwanda became a German Colony in 1895, but after the First World War, in which Germany was defeated, Belgium became the colonial power for Rwanda, and Belgium favoured the Tutsis in the belief (no foundation of course of that belief) that Tutsis were racially superior to Hutus; indeed, Belgium as the colonial power, in reality, preferred the Tutsis, and created favourable conditions for their education, offered them good jobs in the colonial administration. The Tutsi chiefs were entrusted with the task of operating forced labour policies and also ordered corporal punishment for the other race on behalf of the colonial masters.[5] By introducing the system of carrying identification

[5] R Paris, *At War's End: Building Peace After Civil Conflict*, Cambridge, Cambridge University Press (2004).

documents by the Rwandans, the Belgian government, in fact, precipitated the racial classification even further to add to the racial tension.

However, in the 1950s, Rwandans started protesting against their colonial masters. The Hutus, in particular, attempted to overthrow the Tutsi regime with a view to replacing it with a republic which would be led by a president. This time, the Hutu tribe killed hundreds of Tutsis, and looted their homes; eventually, they were made refugees, and they started fleeing the country. A Hutu government was created to rule Rwanda; the Tutsis' attempts to overthrow the Hutu government, even with foreign assistance, failed. Rwanda became an independent State in 1962 with the Hutu government in power.[6]

Rwanda has a large agricultural sector; the income from this sector is quite large; it is also a major coffee producer. In fact, the ruling government encouraged the farmers to produce as much coffee as possible to maintain the government's income. But with the collapse of the International Coffee Agreement, the world coffee market was depressed, and the world prices for coffee were adversely affected. The fall in coffee prices dramatically reduced the country's incomes, the government encountered serious financial crisis, and famines became a common phenomenon throughout the Rwandan countryside. But during this period, Rwanda seems to have mainly survived on foreign and institutional aid.

Meanwhile, a rebel army was formed in Uganda, known as Rwandan Patriotic Front (the Front Patriotique Rwandais—FPR), which required the Rwandan government to spend money in order to fight off the FPR. Indeed, a civil war started with the invasion of FPR. In fact, Tutsis residing in Uganda formed a party with a view to regaining control over Rwanda. The civil war which started in October 1990 lasted for three and a half years. Interestingly enough, this civil war, and the army, were largely funded by some of the States in the West. In October 1994, the Rwandan army started shooting in Kigali, the capital town of Rwanda, and 10,000 Tutsis were imprisoned, and thousands of Tutsis were killed in massacres organised by the national officials in collaboration with the

[6] See further P Uvin, *Development, Aid and Conflict: Reflections from the case of Rwanda*, Working Paper 24, *UN University World Institute for Development Economics Research*, Helsinki (1996).

army and the police.[7] Eltringham's debate on Rwandan Genocide is interesting.[8]

On the other hand, Habyarimana, who ruled Rwanda since 1973 and whose ruling party was known as MRND, used funds obtained from the donors to import about one million machetes which were used in the genocide. It is important to bear in mind that Tutsis, who were thought to be intellectually ahead of the Hutus, had been making various efforts for deepening ethnic hatred similar to the other opposition parties who were also doing the same. But the interesting point remains that before being engaged in this kind of unacceptable conduct one should consider that the consequences of such hatred would contribute to poverty, economic dependence on foreign States and the loss of human resources.

However, it was only in August 1993 that the fighting between the two tribes officially ended, and a UN Peacekeeping Force was sent in within three months of the end of the official fighting. Despite a suggestion put forward by a group of States for a power-sharing agreement between the current regime in Rwanda (Habyarimana government) and the FPR, which proposal eventually came to be known as the Arusha Peace Negotiations, did not, after all, materialise for a variety of reasons, but adverse propaganda against the Tutsis went on. The reigning government did not take much action to suppress the racial hatred within the Rwandan society.

In April 1994, Habyarimana was killed in a plane crash on his way back from Arusha. Violence erupted in Kigali which was predominantly initiated by the presidential guards, but gradually spread to the rest of the country, and obviously, this internal conflict led to the killing of thousands of people.[9] The first UN Peacekeeping Mission failed to work according to the expectation of the UN and indeed the people of Rwanda; the civil war turned so violent that it led to the genocide of 1994.

[7] See further P Uvin, *Development, Aid and Conflict*, op. cit., at 31–32; see also N Eltringham, "Debating the Rwandan Genocide", in P Kaarsholm (ed) *Violence, Political Culture and Development in Africa*, Oxford, Oxford University Press (2006).

[8] See further N Eltringham, "Debating the Rwandan Genocide", op. cit., at 74.

[9] One of the published works in which the massacres in Rwanda has been described very vividly was by P Uvin, *Development, Aid and Conflict*, op. cit., at 32.

The UN Security Council approved a second Peacekeeping Mission to Rwanda, but the government failed to register their willingness to cooperate. In June 1994, France requested another UN mission to Rwanda, which was to be known as Operation Turquoise in order to protect civilians. It contributed very little to settling the internal warfares in Rwanda. However, the civil war ended in the latter part of 1994, but FPR which claimed victory paved the way for a Tutsi government.[10] The Hutus again became the victims of racial hatred.[11]

The Rwandan genocide case was one of the notable cases which was referred to the International Criminal Tribunal for Rwanda (ICTR). But the question remains whether the authoritarian heads of States in the world have learned any lesson from that trial. Most of the internal conflicts that take place in States are racial conflicts in nature, which really should not be allowed by any society.

6.4 Different Faces of Conflicts

Internal conflicts really arise at a national level between different races within a society; but internal conflicts may also arise at a national level when there are nationals of different races in the same country, and each group of people wants the same kind of status, politically and otherwise, in particular, their equal rights to education, religious rights, participation in the political policy-making and so on. In other words, within the society there exists a degree of differentiation between the races, and as stated earlier that such differentiation is based on prejudice, which has no logical basis. There is absolutely no sustainable grounds that one race is better than the other; and this cannot be based on culture, as the term "culture" bears a totally different meaning. It primarily stands for inventive and innovative qualities whether in arts or science or both. By differentiating between races due to prejudices, the society concerned loses human resources, as people of certain races are primarily ostracised in preference to people of other races, and society itself should be held responsible for self-induced differentiation between the races.

[10] See further J M Vaccaro, "The Politics of Genocide: Peace-Keeping and Disaster Relief in Rwanda", in W J Durch (ed), *UN Peacekeeping, American Policy and the Uncivil Wars of the 1990s*, New York, St. Martin's Press (1996) at 369.

[11] Many of the Hutus sought refuge in the UK. See contemporary immigration reports.

In the Rwandan case there was no scientific evidence to establish that people belonging to the Tutsi race are superior to those belonging to the Hutu race, and yet, the prejudice against a race led to an unforgivable genocide. Furthermore, such killings destroyed the country and deepened poverty with its consequential adverse effects.

Racial discrimination when at its peak may lead to a partition of the original country. This is exactly what happened, for example, to India and Yugoslavia. India was divided into two countries to create Pakistan because of religious differences between the Hindus and the Muslims in the main.

The second example to establish what racial hatred can do would be Yugoslavia. President Tito ruled the country peacefully until he died in 1980. Yugoslavia, like India, was a multi-ethnic country, but was kept united in order to avoid Soviet invasion. After the collapse of the Soviet Union, Yugoslavia was entangled in ethnically divided civil war. Interestingly enough, certain ethnically different races began to declare themselves independent as early as 1981 (Tito died in 1980). Gradually, ethnic groups became violent in their efforts to seek independence and the central government's efforts to keep the country united met with failure. However, the attempts made by the central government led to very severe violence, which engulfed almost the entire country, and the violence which was responsible for mass killing in Yugoslavia was also described as another genocide.

The United State of Yugoslavia was effectively dismembered to create the following States—Bosnia and Herzegovina, Croatia, Macedonia, Montenegro, Serbia and Slovenia.[12] Although all ethnic groups in the former Yugoslavia committed atrocities, it was the former president of the country, a Serbian, Slobodan Milosevic, who ruled the country between 1997 and 2000, who was arrested by the then government in 2001 to face the charges of genocide before the International Criminal Tribunal for the former Yugoslavia.[13]

It has already been pointed out that racial hatred which only divided society is a product of prejudice, which should be rationalised, as in effect, there should not be any distinctions between races; it is not biologically rooted. According to Joseph Nye, myths that may be shared by an ethnic

[12] For a very detailed account of the dismemberment of Yugoslavia and how genocide took place, see M Mann, *The Dark Side of Democracy: Explaining Ethnic Cleansing*, Cambridge, Cambridge University Press (2005).

[13] See M Mann, op. cit.

group can change over time.[14] It is believed that prejudices, no matter how deep-rooted they may be, should be overcome by education, rather than believing that they are part of the culture, which idea is totally unfounded.

Is there any politics behind racial hatred which often leads to violent warfares? One theory may be that in poorer countries, this may be a ploy to divert peoples' attention to societal wars to which the government did not contribute; unfortunately, governments fail to appreciate the consequences of their indifference to racial warfares; often foreign powers may be involved in them by providing funds and even weapons.

On the other hand, contrary examples are also available to defy the above-mentioned theory. Yugoslavia was never regarded as a poor country, but it had a genuine societal disharmony owing to the presence of so many people of different races. Whereas President Tito somehow kept the country united, President Milosevic failed to do so, and indeed was accused of genocide in his attempt to bring an end to the societal unrest based on racial inferiority or superiority, as the case may be.

Milosevic-led genocide was unnecessary in that he should have initiated an effective negotiation and/or conciliation process between the leaders of various races within his jurisdiction, which apparently he failed to exhaust thus perpetuating the racial hatred–based unrest within the society.

Hence it may be concluded that racial hatred within societies is simply prejudice-based, which is a deep-rooted perception of people within any jurisdiction. This kind of hatred has no biological roots; it is simply a myth.

6.5 How May Racial Conflicts Be Avoided?

It is to be re-emphasised that racially motivated conflicts/hatred are prejudice-based. Prejudice is a myth, has no scientific basis, is not biologically rooted; nor can it be a part of a culture. In the event of a government being incompetent in promoting the country's economy by creating employment for its people, or enriching the country by setting up industries and by promoting education, the government may indirectly or

[14] J Nye, *Understanding International Conflicts: An Introduction to Theory and History*, New York, Pearson Longman (2005) at 234.

directly instigate racial violence to mask its failure. In such a situation, racial violence may be an inevitable feature of the society concerned.

Interestingly enough, violence, for whatever reason, taking place within a country may have some short-term economic consequences, namely,

- Exploitation of labour by paying very low wages or no wages at all;
- Benefits derived from foreign aid emanating from those countries which have lent sympathy to such violence;
- Exploitation of natural resources after occupying land areas; and
- Exercising control of trade by virtue of raising the price level of exportable goods.[15]

In dealing with domestic violence apparently based on racial hatred, incompetent governments may divert their incompetence to it without appreciating its foreseeable adverse consequences. In recent years, the following countries became victims of racial conflict trap—Afghanistan, Chad, the Congo and South Sudan. Of these four countries, it has been decided to briefly examine the situation in South Sudan.

The undivided Sudan was the largest country on the African continent. Whereas the northern part of Sudan (the capital of which is Khartoum) was predominantly Muslim, the Christians constituted the majority of the population in South Sudan. Some Christians still live in the old capital town. The undivided Sudan was full of natural resources, but the part which had most of the oil fell in the geographic area known as South Sudan. Undivided Sudan seems to have neglected to improve her human resources all along. However, the conflict was fought between the Muslims in the North and the Christians in the South. With the collapse of the coalition between the then president and the other party leaders the latest violence in Sudan started in 2013, although South Sudan became independent in 2011.[16]

The violence in Sudan has a long history at least since 2005—between the two major groups of people—the Muslims and the Christians, so much so that soon after 2005, even the courts in Khartoum had to be separated

[15] See further D Keen, "Incentives and Disincentives for Violence" in M Berdal and D Malone (eds) *Greed and Grievance: Economic Agendas in Civil Wars*, Boulder, Lynne Rienner Publishers (2000) at 26–27.

[16] For a detailed discussion of the situation between the South and the North Sudan, see S P Huntington, *The Clash of Civilisations and the Remaking of World Order*, New York, Simon and Schuster (2011).

whereby a separate court for the Christian community was created in Khartoum. It was at a time when Sudan witnessed severe violence which came to be known as the Darfur Conflict,[17] which lasted for a long period of time.

The conflict which recurred in 2011 was actually three dimensional—the Sudan People's Liberation Movement, a political dispute within the ruling party and a regional and ethnic war. In fact, in both the Sudan People's Liberation Movement and the ethnic war, there was a common element, racial hatred, which as explained before has no logical basis. A Peace Agreement was concluded in August 2015, but unfortunately, it was short-lived. A UN Peacekeeping Mission was stationed in South Sudan, but it is understood that it was mostly engaged in protecting civilians in the UN bases. This racial conflict, it is understood, also killed over a million people. Based on what has been observed above, it may be reiterated that these deaths were totally unnecessary. Furthermore, this conflict could have been ended with fruitful negotiation between the parties concerned without necessitating so many unnecessary deaths. But unfortunately, soon after South Sudan attained its independence in 2011, her main wealth which used to come from the oil sector has changed enormously owing to a variety of factors, namely, more awareness of the general public of the environmental damage, less use of petrol by motor vehicles and more technology-oriented industries, which has reduced the price of petrol very significantly. Unless South Sudan arranges alternative sources of income as a matter of urgency, it is clear that the economy of the country may significantly suffer.

Again, some public awareness programmes are required in an attempt to raise the awareness that racial differences are a matter of prejudice, which has no logical foundation at all. In recent years, Joseph Kony, a self-adorned prophet, savaged villages in Uganda first and thereafter the Congo and South Sudan. He was responsible for the death/killing of more than 100,000 people and kidnapping of 50,000 children; he was accused of genocide and crimes against humanity. In 2005, he was indicted, in absentia, by the International Criminal Court.[18]

[17] See further R Cockett, *Sudan: Darfur and the Failure of an African State*, New Haven, Yale University Press (2010).

[18] See further P Eichstaedt, "Kony 20Never—Inside the Mind of Africa's Most Wanted Men", *Foreign Affairs* (2014).

There is another dimension to these civil wars, that is, in violation of the UN Convention on the Rights of the Child, 1989, the leaders of these rebel groups enticed children into warfares with various promises which would appear to be very attractive, for example, education for free or giving them attractive employment in the future. But this kind of policy to employ child soldiers has far-reaching adverse effect, namely (a) violent warfares may adversely affect a child's psychology; (b) child soldiers are often subject to war-glamorising sessions, which may not be true at all; the inevitable atrocity of any soldier of any age is to kill the enemies; and (c) they are never told that these warfares are occasioned by racial hatred which has no sustainable grounds to support these warfares. Often the leaders of racial hatred groups do not explain the truth to children why their services would be necessary. Children often glamorise servicing the army as many of the members of their families were members of the armed forces. But national armed forces are different from armed forces constituted of children, who are underage to join any type of forces. Often children, in the event of their showing reluctance to joining the forces, are threatened with revenge on their parents or other close relatives in the families; the leaders' principal aim is to entice them by glamorising warfares—that by joining the children army, the members of which are less than 18 years of age, they are assured of good food on a daily basis and good wages which they would not dream of earning anywhere in the country.[19]

Racial conflicts have very deep-seated roots in the world. It may not be avoided too quickly. Those who are at the root of these conflicts have to appreciate, perhaps mostly by training, that there are no biological differences between races and that there are no other forms of differences between races.

6.6 Conclusions

Knowledge in negotiating techniques in ending armed conflicts is an issue which should be learned by the leaders of the racial hatred–based domestic warfares for the following main reasons: (a) that these warfares are

[19] See further R Brett and I Specht, *Young Soldiers: Why They Choose to Fight*, Boulder, Lynne Rienner Publishers (2004); see also UNICEF *At Least 65,000 Children Released from Armed Forces and Groups over the Last 10 Years—UNICEF News Release*, New York and Paris (2017).

domestic in nature and it is for the ruling governments to take the initiative to end them; (b) on the other hand, as has been explained in this chapter that the domestic governments owing to their incompetence in running their governments to protect the interests of their people, who installed them in power, often drive their people into such warfares. Diplomats will hardly have anything to negotiate these warfares, as they are solely domestic in nature, although these warfares may be strengthened by certain external States primarily by and through financial aid or by providing weapons. National diplomats may not have any locus standi to negotiate these warfares.

It is for the leaders who initiate these warfares on unfounded grounds to learn and propagate that there are no biological differences between races. In the final analysis, they will not be able to justify their acts, although they should be held responsible for untold miseries they create and very large number of human beings they kill in these unnecessary warfares.

There hardly exists any society in our time which is not multi-racial. People are now required to learn to live in such societies irrespective of their countries of origin, their religious faith, their complexion and so on, otherwise, any racial discriminations practised by the people in any society will not only contribute to causing unnecessary warfare which has no mentionable merits, in addition to losing human resources in that society.

CHAPTER 7

Negotiating Techniques in Arranging Project Finance and Syndicated Loan Agreements

7.1 Introduction

Project finance is not a novel concept, but it has in recent years attained a degree of complexity, and this is particularly owing to the changing business environment. The business world is, in general, unpredictable and very conscious of securities against any lending. In the past, trust in a business entity or even in a commercial man was enough to lend money to the business or to the commercial man. But the contemporary business world is full of risks, and these have received attention in a separate section of this chapter.

Project financing plans vary from finance house to finance house. In this chapter, an attempt is made to examine the common features, including the main clauses that are usually incorporated into project finance proposals, irrespective of the nature of the business for which finance may be sought.

Syndicated loans have become a major source of finance for various projects. The mechanism of syndicated loan has also been briefly examined in this chapter.

Projecting finance is a sophisticated version of a project for borrowing preferably by corporate entities because against this type of financing large security by the borrower would be necessary. Project financing system has been with the business community since the beginning of the twentieth century, perhaps to a certain extent, owing to the de-localisation process

C. Chatterjee, *Negotiating Techniques in Diplomacy and Business Contracts*, https://doi.org/10.1007/978-3-030-81732-9_7

many of the newly born countries attracted private foreign investors, mainly in the form of transnational corporations. Additionally, after the Second World War, both France and Germany were engaged in re-building their economy, hence demands for additional finance sources increased.

Although it has a long history, the growth and development of this method of raising finance were rather haphazard. Of course, one is required to remind oneself that the world of private foreign investments was not appropriately mapped out until the 1970s when the oil crisis was triggered by the advent of the Arab-Israeli differences and gained a new height; as a consequence new risks in the world of private foreign investments turned up resulting in even more uncertainty. The developing countries, in particular, were required to offer appropriate assurances against the consequences of risks. Investors in the Western world necessarily became weary of the developing world, in general, about making investments in that part of the world.

Furthermore, many of the private foreign investors developed a high level of hesitancy in making large investments in the developing countries, as during the first two or three decades after the de-colonisation process started, a heavy cloud of uncertainty hung over the conduct of some of the sovereign States. But, fortunately, the cloud seems to have disappeared now.

Project financing must pay attention to the risks involved in lending the funds applied for. This issue has received attention in a separate section of this chapter.

It should be emphasised at the outset that both project financing and syndicated loan arrangements are really meant for providing finance for various projects; lawyers simply follow either the standard contracts developed by themselves or other forms of standard contract. The primary purpose of this chapter is to familiarise the reader with the basic issues arising under project financing and syndicated loan arrangements. Once the finance people have negotiated the terms of finance under either of the forms, lawyers simply complete the standard contracts.

7.2 What Is Project Finance?

It stands for a technique of raising finance for projects which may contribute to developing the economy of the country, whether by developing the agricultural or industrial or education sector. This method may also raise finance for capital projects in a country, such as energy-related or mining.

No lender may be prepared to lend any fund without a guarantee that it will be repaid with interest on it, by the stipulated period of time.

Borrowers are usually of two types: public and private. In the case of a public or State borrower, risks do not present much of a problem other than the change or abolition of the public entity; and in that event the government remains responsible, and if the government changes, then the successor government will remain responsible for the repayment of the loan, and this may be secured by incorporating a succession clause into the loan agreement.

Where however the borrower is a private entity, irrespective of its size, risks in regard to repayment becomes a worrying problem, unless security against the loan offered by the borrower has been accepted by the lender. Promises for repayment of the loan with interest thereon by others may not be accepted by the lenders. This is an issue for the borrower and the lender to settle and incorporate into the loan agreement.

When a public body plans to borrow funds from an international organisation, such as the International Bank for Reconstruction and Development (IBRD—the World Bank) or the International Development Association (IDA), it must ensure that it is a member of that organisation and also that the fund is sought for a programme which would contribute to the socio-economic development of that country. The onus is on the prospective borrowing entity to satisfy the lending institution concerned. Often, in such borrowing, capacity-building of the country's human resources becomes a condition to it, and it is for the borrowing country to satisfy the prospective lending organisation on this issue.

7.3 Certain Essentials of Project Finance[1]

7.3.1 Project Profile

A project profile stands for the description of the perceived project. It should be developed in a simple and yet comprehensive way; it must also be developed without using jargon unless in regard to technical issues where the use of jargon proves to be essential. It must include all possible details of the project in order to enable the lenders to conceptualise it

[1] See further S K Chatterjee, "Procedural Aspects of Project Finance", 10 *Journal of International Business Law*, 1993, at 421.

correctly. Nothing should be left to the imagination of the prospective lenders.

It is also important for the borrower to disclose all the foreseeable problems that may arise from the contemplated project, in addition to providing the information as to what materials might be made available to the private foreign investors and also whether any local human resources might be made available to them. Otherwise, in the event of providing any misleading information on the proposed project which might cause delay in completing the project in consequence of which the project owner would be required to incur more than the estimated costs. In that event the lenders might decline more funds unless, of course, there really occurs certain unforeseeable event. All these risks should be insured against; in fact, a prudent lender would ask for such a policy.

Borrowers' responsibilities under a project finance scheme can be very extensive indeed. On the other hand, lenders also have to go by their codes of conduct prevalent on the market and the relevant laws in the jurisdiction. They would also be required to comply with the conditions of lending, both legislative or otherwise, in lending money to any project in a foreign jurisdiction. There will arise the additional risks if the borrower and lender change, hence the importance of a succession clause in a lending and borrowing agreement. However, whether the prospective lender is its own bank or an external lender, the borrower will be required to submit usually three months' bank statements to the prospective lender.

Although bank lending a large sum of money is usually governed by the central bank of the country in which the commercial bank is located, lending by private lending institutions is not governed by any central bank, but as an investment bank it will be regulated by its regulatory body too, unless the borrower is a public entity. All large borrowings will be subject to security, and this is where projects for which finance is to be raised by private borrowers, particularly large borrowings, are presented with hurdles, which sometimes may prove to be difficult to resolve. Some borrowers may come up with one asset or two as security; it is for the lenders to decide whether to accept such securities or not.

Third-party undertakings may also present difficulties in that the lenders may decline to accept third-party offers; furthermore, the third party concerned must have substantial assets to give undertakings and those assets must be frozen until the debt accrued by the borrower has been extinguished. However, third-party undertakings may be accepted by lenders, but it would be a difficult deal to achieve, and neither the borrower nor the third party who may have shown its interest to provide security will hardly have any room for negotiation. The prospective borrower, if the amount of borrowing is rather large, may try syndications, but it may be difficult to break the barrier with them too. It may be an idea for a private borrower to borrow a relatively large amount of money against its own security from its own bank, which would be based on the regularity of payments; then the prospective borrower might stand a better chance to borrow a larger amount in the future. But it must be pointed out that one should not take for granted what had been written for the position of a prospective borrower vis-à-vis its bank. Every case is different from a lender's perspective.

7.3.2 Public Borrowers

Most of the States or State-sponsored bodies borrow on a regular basis with a view to meeting their expenses on various programmes. No security is usually necessary for government borrowing; however, in the contract, there will be included in the loan agreement a succession clause in order to ensure that the debt obligation is passed on to the successor government.

Indeed, historical examples exist whereby the successor governments or newly de-colonised countries refused to accept the debts incurred by their colonial powers, namely, Algeria refused to succeed the debts accrued by France, her former colonial power. But these examples are simply anecdotal. There are a few examples of this kind of behaviour on the part of certain States in the recent history of the world. It may safely be assumed that States in the contemporary world would hesitate to misbehave themselves in the financial world—the primary sources of borrowing being the International Monetary Fund (IMF) which really extends funds to its Member States in order to enable them to correct their adverse balance of payments; but most of the developing countries will seek loans mainly from the IDA, which is an association under the World Bank Group. IMF loans are usually for a short period of time unless extension of time for repayment is granted by the IMF authorities.

In summary, public entities are safer borrowers than private entities. One should not forget the collapse of Enron or Merrill Lynch. Governments do not go into liquidation. But lending to the government of a rather poor economy would be quite risky. Incidentally, poor countries should urgently develop a reliable banking system, a discussion of which would be beyond the remit of this work. Both borrower and lender should be aware of the fact that country profiles on each country, preferably members of the World Bank, are available from the website of the World Bank.

7.3.3 *Lending and Borrowing*

Like most other businesses, lending and borrowing of money are also a business which entails earnings or losses of money. Both the parties should therefore be cautious of the risks they are undertaking in this business. It has already been explained that in detailing the project, the prospective borrowers should also list the risks they are aware of in relation to the project on which they seek funding. The fact remains that the local bank should be the borrower's first port of call for borrowing funds. Only if their efforts should fail at that level, should they seek borrowing from external sources, including syndications which have briefly received attention in the latter part of this chapter.

Depending on the performance of the borrower, the lender(s) may impose conditions on the borrower in order to recover their money. On the other hand, if the lenders decide to wind up their business for whatever reason, who may be the next provider? This issue should particularly be incorporated into the lending agreement. This problem is occasioned between two private parties.

It has already been stated in this chapter that in the event of a sovereign authority being succeeded by a subsequent sovereign authority, the succession clause in the loan agreement should come to the rescue of the borrower.

Loan agreements are usually long-term agreements; thus, the question remains, what would happen to a loan agreement if the territory of the former sovereign is ceded to another sovereign entity? The answer to this question would be that loan agreements are not "treaties"; thus, these agreements are not governed by the Vienna Convention on the Law of Treaties 1969, although the legal position on this matter would have been different if obligations arose under development aid agreements[2] to which

[2] These agreements are treated as *sui generis* in character or as quasi-international agreements. See further A Vedross "Quasi-international agreements and International Economic Transactions", 18 *Year Book of International Affairs* (1964) at 230. It is re-iterated that for loan agreements concluded between a private party and a sovereign entity, successor governments remain liable to honour the obligations of their predecessors.

an international organisation is a party and the obligations thereunder devolve on successor governments.

The issue of succession, unification, cessions and so on are currently dealt with by the Vienna Convention on Succession of States in Respect of Treaties 1978. The caution should be entered that although the principle of *pacta sunt servanda* is quite regularly observed particularly in the Western world, no one can predict how a sovereign government might act on this issue. Loan agreements to which governments are parties should be concluded on behalf of the State concerned; if that government and State become non-existent, and then if the new State and the government decline to pay any money borrowed by the former government of that geographic area, nothing may be done about it.

In the *Tinoco* Arbitration,[3] while ruling Costa Rica as a dictator, Tinoco granted concessions to certain British companies, and certain bank notes. The government which deposed Tinoco declared that the concessions and bank notes which Tinoco respectively granted and issued were invalid. The dispute was referred to a sole arbitrator, who decided that although Tinoco's government was regarded as unconstitutional under Costa Rican law and was not recognised by many foreign governments, including that of Great Britain, Tinoco's acts were binding on the successor government. Obviously, the successor government found it difficult to comprehend the rationale of the arbitrator's award. The lesson that investors may like to derive from the arbitrator's award is that they should not perhaps conclude a long-term investment or commercial contract with a government considered unconstitutional under the local law. That kind of act would be regarded as an invitation to risks.

On the other hand, many foreign investors might feel persuaded by charismatic heads of States to invest in his/her territory; but this may also prove to be risky. The successor might not accept the obligations incurred by the former government, and the investors' position becomes very uncertain.[4] However, finance lent to a public body by any institution,

[3](1923) 1 UNRIAA 369.

[4]See SEDCO Inc. v Iranian Oil Co and the Islamic Republic of Iran, Iran-US Claims Tribunal, Award of 24 October 1985, 27 March 1986 and 2 July 1987, 84 *International Law Reports* (1991) 484; see also Mobil Oil Iran Inc. and Others v Government of the Islamic Republic of Iran and the National Iranian Oil Co and Others v Government of the Islamic Republic of Iran and National Iranian Oil Co (Award No 311—74/76/81/150—3), 86 *International Law Reports* (1991) 231.

private, public or even an international organisation, becomes a national debt,[5] and successor government will remain liable for the debt until it is settled.[6]

One final issue to consider in the context of this section of the chapter would be the position of debtor (public) when it may lose that part of the territory where the project is located, and the debt was incurred in regard to that project. One answer to this issue would be that the original debtor carries the debt with it/him, but that would be an impractical answer. The debtor should discuss this issue with the new owner of the project and with the consent of the new head of the ceded territory the debt should be passed to the new head of the project with the consent of the lender(s).[7] Incidentally, during the de-colonisation period, the debts of the colonial powers passed on to the newly born States, although a few of them refused to accept them.[8]

Ministry/department for whose work the loan is being applied for should be clearly stated unless of course the central government itself has made the application in relation to a project for the country. In both instances, parliamentary approval to the proposed project and the amount of borrowing approved by it should be attached to the proposal for raising the loan.

7.3.4 The Project

Irrespective of whether the prospective borrower is a private corporation or a public body, the proposed project on which funds may be sought must be detailed as much as possible. This is one of the principal works that the prospective borrowers must complete, and ensure that the description of the project is absolutely clear to the prospective lenders too. The stages through which the project is to be completed and the drawings of the project must be clear to understand by anybody engaged in lending and borrowing funds.

[5] See further Kleitis v Republic of Austria, Ann. Digest (1948) Case No 18.

[6] See further *Dass v Secretary of State for India in Council* (1875) LR 19.

[7] *Chilliov France* (*The Grano Case*), UN Report vol. xv at 77; see also H Cahn, "The Responsibility of the Successor State for War Debts", 44 *American Journal of International Law* (1950) at 477.

[8] See further the Peace Treaty with Italy 1947, UNTS, vol. 49 at 126; see also the Case of Burma, now Myanmar, Cmnd 7360.

The purposes of the project should also be clearly stated; and in what way(s) it might contribute to the economy, when completed; the borrower should confirm whether the project would need any foreign experts to check it, and if so, the duration of their services and the probable costs involved in it.

In drafting the project on which finance is being sought, alternative project ideas should also be suggested with costs of completion of those projects too, in order to enable the prospective lenders to work out their own costs-benefits analysis.

It would be appreciated if the authors of the project (the applicant borrower(s)) could also explain whether the proposed project would entail any capacity-building element whereby in the future such projects would not require the assistance of any foreign experts. The government department or the State agency concerned will also be required to satisfy all the above-mentioned conditions.

The proposed project shall not be such which would be beyond the capacity of the project initiators. All projects are supposed to be completed in all their major aspects by their own people. It would be important to bear in mind that the lenders might be more willing to lend money if only they are satisfied that the project, when completed, would be beneficial for the country and also that the local people would be able to look after the project, including its maintenance.

7.3.5 Availability of Finance

Usually, the granted finance is made available through instalments. It is also usually provided in US dollars, a currency which fluctuates quite often; thus, it would be advisable to have the rate of exchange fixed between the US dollar and the currency of the beneficiary country. This eventually becomes a term of the loan agreement too. The date by which the loan will be settled must also be noted in the loan agreement along with the rate of interest *per annum*. Usually, the lenders do not show much enthusiasm in lending money in the country's own currency, unless of course, the currency is a hard one.

7.3.6 The Default Clause

This clause is often called the "disaster clause." If, for any reason, a borrower should fail to return the agreed money, perhaps in instalments, by the stipulated date, the lenders will have the right to terminate the loan agreement, unless of course the borrower notifies the lenders with sustainable justifications, but must bear in mind that in paying the "default" amount back, the borrower may have to pay a "penalty" to be suggested by the lenders, together with interest thereon as from the due date of payment of the failed instalment.

The borrowers should bear in mind that the lenders have the right to cancel the entire loan if any default occurs. This should be clearly stated in the default clause in the loan agreement.

7.3.7 The Issue of Sovereign Immunity

As explained before, if the borrower is a public entity (the government itself) or a State entity, by virtue of being a sovereign or its subsidiary, the public entity in its variety of forms will claim State immunity if any court proceedings for whatever reason are brought against it by the lenders. But the lenders' best form of security against their loan would be to incorporate a succession clause into the loan agreement. This only applies to public entities, that is, the government or a government entity. What it means is that by incorporating a State immunity clause into the related loan agreement, the government and/or the public entity may be immune to any form of court proceedings or otherwise.

The concept of State immunity has been with the international community for a very long time. It is closely connected to the concept of "absolute sovereignty." However, with the changing climate of the commercial world not only within the UK jurisdiction but also worldwide, the concept of absolute sovereignty or the inviolability of the State immunity has been subject to various controversies.[9]

[9] A number of very good published works on this topic are available, namely, H Fox and P Webb, *The Law of State Immunity*, Oxford, Oxford University Press, latest edition; S Sucharitkul, *State Immunity and Trading Activities in International Law*, Leiden (1959); S Sinclair, "The Law of Sovereign Immunity: Recent Developments", 167 Hague Recueil (1980) at 113; A Aust, "The Law of State Immunity" 53 *International and Comparative Law Quarterly* 2004 at 255, R Higgins, "Certain Unresolved Aspects of the Law of State Immunity", 29 *Netherlands International Law Review* (1982) at 265; Oppenheim's

In the context of this work there is no need to detail the historical growth and development of sovereign immunity. In the olden days when the concept of "sovereignty" was cited by the French political thinker Bodin, it stood for "all powerful," "omnipotent" and not amenable to anybody. Indeed, public international law recognised the principle of "sovereign equality," a principle on which the UN was also set up. But immunity was originally allowed to heads of States, and thereafter their diplomats, who are governed by the Vienna Convention on Diplomatic Relations, 1961; then came the Vienna Convention on Consular Relations, 1963, to govern the conduct of consular officers of various categories. Both diplomats and consular officers are representatives of their sovereign.

The concept of sovereign immunity was gradually extended to include commercial transactions, also when a public entity was involved in it, but not foreign sovereigns. The notable case on this issue, that is, there must exist a relationship between territorial jurisdiction and sovereign immunity, was *The Schooner Exchange v McFaddon*[10] in which case the claimants alleged that they were the sole owners of the Exchange which sailed in 1809 from Baltimore to Spain.

She was seized in December 1810 on the basis of decrees issued by Napoleon. They alleged that no sentence had been pronounced against her by any competent court and that an order for the restitution of the vessel be issued which was then lying at Philadelphia. The US Attorney for the District of Pennsylvania filed a recommendation suggesting that since peace subsisted between the US and Napoleon, public vessels of the latter might enter and leave US ports without any interference.

The District Court dismissed the libel, but that decision was reversed by the Circuit Court; however, the US Supreme Court restored the original decision. Marshall CJ stated, inter alia, that:

> ... perfect equality and absolute independence of sovereigns, and this common interest impelling them to mutual intercourse, and an interchange of good offices with each other, have given rise to a class of cases in which every sovereign is understood to waive the exercise of a part of that complete

International Law vol. I, R Y Jennings and A D Watts, Oxford, Oxford University Press (1992) at 341; and C H Schreuer, *State Immunity: Some Recent Developments*, Cambridge, Cambridge University Press (1988).

[10] Supreme Court of the United States (1812) 7 Cranch 116.

exclusive territorial jurisdiction, which has been stated to be the attributes of every nation.[11]

In the *Cristina* case[12] the Members of the House of Lords aired different opinions as to the application of the immunity rules. Cristina, which was a Spanish vessel, registered at Bilbao, was at the material time lying at Cardiff. However, prior to her arrival at Cardiff, the respondents, the Government of the Spanish Republic, passed a decree whereby all Spanish vessels registered at Bilbao would be requisitioned. The original owners of Cristina (the appellants in this case) initiated an action by a writ *in rem* claiming that as the sole owners of the vessel they be allowed possession of her. The Spanish government entered a conditional appearance and gave notice of motion for the dismissal of the action.

The Court of first instance, the Court of Appeal and the House of Lords found in favour of the Spanish government a foreign sovereign State. Lord Wright said:

> ... [There are] general principles of international law according to which a sovereign State is held to be immune from the jurisdiction of another sovereign State. This is sometimes said to flow from international comity or courtesy, but may now more properly be regarded as a rule of international law, accepted among the community of nations. It is binding on the municipal courts of this country in the sense and to the extent that it has been received and enforced by these courts.[13]

The following are also some of the important cases in which absolute immunity was granted by the English courts:

(a) Parlement Belge[14]
(b) Porto Alexandre[15]
(c) The Cristina[16]
(d) Duff Development Company v Kelantan[17]

[11] Reproduced in L C Green, *International Law Through the Cases*, London, Stevens & Sons Ltd. at 266.

[12] [1938] AC 485.

[13] See further L C Green, op. cit., at 284.

[14] (1880) 5 PD 197.

[15] [1920] P 30.

[16] [1938] AC 485.

[17] [1924] AC 797.

(e) *Baccus SRL* v *Servicio Nacional del Trigo*[18]

It would be appropriate to mention in this context that in *Porto Alexandre*, two of the Lords criticised the decision on the grounds that it was doubtful whether State trading vessels would be eligible for absolute sovereign immunity.[19]

The *Porto Alexandre* must have indicated that absolute immunity may not be allowed in all cases in which the State would be somehow involved. In other words, the days of restrictive immunity was looming large on the horizon.

One of the early attempts on the issue was made by the Brussels Convention on the Immunity of State-owned Ships, 1926, which examined the position of such vessels, which, in reality, carried on non-State trading activities with the increased involvement of States or public entities. This movement got momentum and again in 1952, through its Tate Letter, the US State Department confirmed the increasing involvement of public entities in commercial activities and in consequence, the State Department decided to follow the restrictive theory of sovereign immunity.[20] Indeed, the Tate Letter was a timely letter when one thinks of one of the effects of de-colonisation of the former colonies; most of the commercial activities attracting private foreign investments are carried out in the name of the State government or a public entity under it. The restrictive immunity approach received the support from the US Supreme Court judges in *Alfred Dunhill of London Inc. v Republic of Cuba*.[21] The *Cristina* case should be regarded as a turning point for the English courts. The climax of all this was reached in *Trendtex Trading Corporation Ltd. v Central Bank of Nigeria*.[22] The Anglo-American judicial initiatives on the issue of granting restrictive immunity when a State or public entity would be involved in commercial activities gained ground so much so that many other countries, namely Australia, Canada, Pakistan, Singapore and South Africa, changed their policy on this issue too. There are quite a number of countries that do not agree to the restrictive approach to sovereign immunity on the grounds that restrictive sovereign immunity doctrine is based

[18] [1957] 1 QB 438.

[19] [1938] AC 485 at 490.

[20] 26 Department of State 984 (1952).

[21] 15 ILM [1976] at 735.

[22] [1977] 2 WLR 356; see also *1o Congreso del Partido* [1981] 2 ALL ER 1064; and *Alcom Ltd. v Republic of Colombia* [1984] 2 ALL ER 6.

on judicial decisions and not any executive act. But what will be the legal and judicial position if a State entity becomes a party to a dispute concerned with the issue whether or not to rely on absolute immunity in a jurisdiction which believes in restrictive immunity? One may also hope that in these days of transnational activities, in which State entities are involved, these countries will soon review their position on this issue.

In 1976, the US government formalised its position on the issue of restrictive immunity by enacting the Foreign Sovereign Immunities Act. The UK government followed suit and in 1978 the government passed the UK State Immunity Act. Section 3(1) of the State Immunity Act provides that a State is not immune to proceedings relating to:

(a) a commercial transaction entered into by the State; or
(b) an obligation of the State which by virtue of a contract (whether a commercial transaction or not) falls to be performed wholly or partly in the UK.

S.3(3) of the State Immunity Act 1978 defined the term "commercial transaction" in the following way:

(a) any contract for the supply of goods or services;
(b) any loan or other transaction for the provision of finance and any guarantee or indemnity in respect of any such transaction or of any other financial obligation; and
(c) any other transaction or activity (whether of a commercial, industrial, financial, professional or other similar character) into which a State enters or in which it engages otherwise than in the exercise of sovereign authority.

The provisions of both S.3(1) and S.3(3) may provoke controversy. What is a "commercial transaction" may have to be defined in every case by referring to the commercial character of activity rather than its purpose.

Incidentally, S.1603(d) of the Foreign Sovereign Immunities Act 1976 defined "commercial activity" as a "regular course of commercial conduct or a particular transaction or act."

Nevertheless, the question remains what would be the precise distinction between a "commercial transaction" and a "transaction entered into by a State in the exercise of its sovereign authority"? Again, perhaps the answer would lie in the nature of the transaction even when it is entered into by a State in the exercise of its sovereign authority.

Based on the above discussion, it may be observed that in many instances it may be different from a legal standpoint to determine a clear-cut distinction between *actus jure imperii* and *acta jure imperii*, bearing in mind that a sovereign State, as Sir Gerald Fitzmaurice maintained, remains as such; it does not cease to be sovereign even when it performs acts which a private citizen might perform.[23]

Both the UK State Immunity Act 1978 and the US Foreign Sovereign Immunities Act 1976 respectively define "commercial transactions" and "commercial activity" but both of them fail to identify the legal problems that these two terms present. The US Statute refers to "commercial activity" whereas the UK Statute refers to "commercial transactions"; the term "commercial activity" is wider than "commercial transactions"; however, this difference does not answer the question whether "commercial transactions" or "commercial activities" usually lead to a binding contract between the parties concerned. The vagueness of these terms was rightly identified by Higgins:

> A contract for sale and purchase is to be regarded as a commercial transaction, an actas jure gestionis, but what about a contract to purchase missiles?[24]

Missiles are usually purchased by public entities for national security purposes. Can a contract for sale and purchase of missiles be regarded as a commercial activity or transaction? It has already been pointed out that under the US Act 1976 it is the nature of the activity that matters, rather than its purpose. Thus, under the US Foreign Sovereign Immunities Act 1976 purchase and sale of missiles would be regarded as a "commercial activity."

Returning to the discussion of project finance and syndicated loan agreements, it may be maintained that if either of the transactions takes place within the sovereign jurisdiction of the US, then either of these transactions may be regarded simply as examples of commercial activities; the definition of the term "commercial transaction" in the UK State Immunity Act 1978 appears in Section 3 of the Act.

[23] G Fitzmaurice, "State Immunity from Proceedings in Foreign Courts", (1933) 14 *British Year Book of International Law*, 101 at 121.

[24] R Higgins, *Problems & Processes, International Law and How We Use It*, Oxford, Oxford University Press (1995) at 82.

As Lord Diplock pointed out in *Alcom v Republic of Colombia*[25] that the State Immunity Act failed to see the grey area between *acta jure imperii* and *acta juris gestionis*. In choosing the jurisdiction whether for project finance or for syndicated loans, the entrepreneurs may bear in mind the issues raised in the above section of this chapter.

7.3.8 Succession Clause

This clause also binds the successor government; that is, in the event of the borrowing government or one of its State entities that borrowed the money being deposed by another government, the successor government will remain liable to pay-off the loan. This is a very important protective clause for the lenders.

This clause is not available to corporate entity borrowers; hence the issue of security becomes important for them, and whatever security the lenders may have accepted against the risks for providing the loan; in the event of the borrower failing to discharge its liability, claim will be served by the lenders on the security holders, or the failed corporate borrower will be required to sell the properties or assets and pay off the debt out of the proceeds of the sale of those properties and other assets too, if necessary. The lenders will have the first charge on those properties and/or assets too.

7.3.9 Periodic Reports

It is common practice of lenders to seek periodic reports on the progress made on the project on which funds were granted. In the event of the borrower failing to reach the target of the stipulated debt, it will be required to justify its failure with sustainable reasons. If however the reasons provided by the borrower are not found to be reasonable by the lenders, that decision by the lenders might risk the loan too. It might therefore be prudent on the part of the borrower to raise the issue initially orally with the lenders and thereafter formalise it in writing.

[25] [1984] 2 All ER 6.

7.4 Risk Study in Relation to Syndicated Loans

This is very much a matter for the lending institutions, be they finance houses, or syndications for lending money. Every institution has its own method of studying risks.

However, when the prospective borrower is a private entity, it may be rather difficult to ascertain the real risks in relation to a private entity; the merits of carrying out "due diligence" on corporate entities often prove to be a mere formality. But, nevertheless, it has become a general practice to carry out "due diligence" on private entities with a view to ascertaining risks for lending purposes.

In so far as proposals for lending finance to public bodies are concerned, the lender(s) may like to look up the most recent country profile of the country concerned from the website of the World Bank (the International Bank for Reconstruction and Development—IBRD). This country profile would identify almost every important political and economic information of the country concerned. This information should enable the lenders whether loan sought for may be extended to the applicant government or not.

In the process of risk study, one should not bear any bias in favour or against a country. There seems to exist a rather old perception that developing countries are riskier than developed countries, which perception may be based on prejudices. In reality, the developed countries are riskier for investment than the developing countries. For example, developed countries have the following risks, namely, high tax regimes, environmental risks, intellectual property-related risks, industrial relations risks, volatile property market risks, high wages risks, to name but a few. But one should maintain that the political regimes in the West, in general, are predictable and less volatile. Furthermore, the judicial system in England is regarded as the most impartial one in the world by virtue of being separable and separate from the executive.

Of course, in the case of a debtor being a public body, the risks for losing money would be minimal, if a succession clause is incorporated into the loan agreement. This issue has been discussed again in a separate section of this chapter.

Risk study is not to be governed by any human perception; it should be based on actual facts which may be ascertained by referring to the conduct of a borrower over the past few years. No lender should think of lending money to a borrower the financial records of which do not warrant it. Risk study must be fact-based; but unfortunately, sometimes not all information provided by the prospective borrower may be verifiable, and sometimes it may genuinely be very difficult to provide evidence in support of some of the information provided by a prospective borrower; and this is where the lenders are required to rationalise their decision on an application for a large amount of borrowing.

The market volatility in regard to the business in which a private borrower is engaged is an important factor which should be considered by prospective lenders; public entity borrowers, on the other hand, usually borrow not for profit-making but for completing specific projects in the interest of the country concerned, and the objectives of a public entity may not be questioned.

However, reputable private corporate entities render an invaluable service to the community, and they also spread their business across national boundaries. They also add to the wealth of the nation. Thus both types of borrowers' merits should be considered from a pragmatic point of view in considering their applications for loans. The objectives for which a loan is to be raised are important factors which should be taken into consideration in determining the merits and weaknesses of a loan application irrespective of whether it has been submitted by a private entity or a public entity.

7.5 Organisation of Syndicates

A syndicate in the context of this chapter is a club of lenders who have registered their interests in considering the loan application whether it is made by a private or a public entity. It must be assumed that when an application is made for quite a large amount of loan and when that loan may not be extended by any one lender, in the commercial practice, a syndicate, a club of prospective lenders, is constituted. Each of the members of a syndicate is usually very experienced in examining financial and related risks. It must be ensured however that no member of the syndicate who has any connection with the applicant, direct or indirect, is chosen, as otherwise, they may be suspected of bias in favour or against the applicant.

The location of the syndication should be carefully chosen, as ideally, the law of the location should be the governing law of the loan agreement. This issue may be controversial in that the loan provider might insist on having their chosen law as the governing law of the loan agreement. This issue has received further attention under the sub-item Dispute Settlement. However, there is no harm for the applicant borrower to justify with reason why they should support or reject the lenders' choice of the governing law of the loan agreement. Each syndicate should be headed by the nominated member.

7.6 Some of the Primary Clauses Which Are Traditionally Incorporated into a Syndicated Loan Agreement

It would be important to bear in mind that although syndicated loan agreements are primarily a bilateral agreement, they are *sui generis* in character; that is, this kind of agreement should not be confused with any other agreements/contracts—it is, in fact, a multi-party agreement, and yet its governing law will be the law chosen by the borrower and the lenders. From this point of view, it is regarded as a bilateral agreement/contract. The parties to a syndicate will be regarded as one party, as the borrower(s) will be regarded as another party. Like all other contracts, a syndicated loan agreement/contract is also based on the principle of good faith, *uberrimae fidei*. In this section, this instrument has been described as an agreement rather than a contract, as the term "agreement" is used in the financial/commercial world in describing these contracts. The language of the agreement should be as simple as possible. There hardly exists any room for negotiation for the borrowers.

7.6.1 The Preamble

The Preamble to an agreement/contract is fundamentally important as it should briefly state the objectives of the instrument, and judicial bodies refer to this clause, when necessary. In the Preamble, therefore, the purposes/objectives for which the loan is granted should be clearly stated, whether the borrower is a public entity or a private entity. Itemisation of the objectives should be clearly identifiable, and the lenders may keep an eye on them whether the loan money is actually being utilised for those objectives.

7.6.2 *The Parties*

The private party or the public party, as the case may be, must clearly state their names and addresses of their headquarters/head office and the location(s) of their offices which may be directly or indirectly involved in raising the funds. In addition to giving its name in full, if the private entity had been registered, it must include its registration number, and the location of its registration must be clearly stated in the loan agreement. In the case of a transnational corporation, the name and the location of the headquarters, including its registration number, names of branches, subsidiaries, wholly owned or otherwise, and their addresses too must be included in the agreement. The company's special meeting that has approved the borrowing, its resolution should be attached too. The same procedure shall also apply if the corporation/company is not a transnational corporation/company.

In the case of a public entity, the official title of the government, with a mention of its capital town, and a brief description of the project on which they plan to raise finance should be clearly stated on the proposal.

7.6.3 *Responsibilities of the Members of a Syndicate*

Each member of the syndicate (usually banks) remains individually and collectively liable to provide the agreed amount of money to the borrowers, and for each of the agreed instalments on a stipulated date. In the event of the syndicate failing to provide the agreed amount of funds to the borrower on the stipulated date, the borrower(s) will have the right to bring a claim against the syndicate. This is because the borrower(s) agree to pay the workers and other members of the project on a particular date, and in the event of the borrower(s) failing to pay each of them on that date, the employees and workers at all levels will have the right to bring claims against the borrower(s); in consequence of which the project may not be completed on the originally stipulated date.

The syndicate therefore undertakes a special obligation towards its borrower(s) on this issue. In fact, the lenders and/or the syndicate should individually and collectively give a written undertaking to the borrower(s) on this issue, including its liability in the event of its failure to provide the funds on the stipulated date(s).

7.6.4 The Issue of Force Majeure

In the world of law, risks are of four types: foreseen, unforeseen, foreseeable and unforeseeable. English courts may consider only unforeseeable risks; and this may be established by referring to some of the decided cases, for example:

(a) See statements made by Lord Radcliffe in Davis Contractors Ltd v Fareham UDC[26]
(b) Metropolitan Water Board v Dick, Kerr & Co[27]
(c) Tsakiroglou & Co Ltd. v Noblee Thorl GmbH[28] (The Suez Canal Cases)
(d) The Chrysalis[29]
(e) Atisa SA v Aztec AG[30]

One of the basic principles of the Law of Contract is the principle of "Good Faith," which contracting parties should strictly adhere to. If the loan agreement states that the governing law of it is English law, then the English courts' attitude towards *force majeure* should be borne in mind. Therefore neither the borrower nor the lenders may invoke *force majeure* on the grounds which the courts in England and Wales may find unsustainable. In fact, it may be difficult for both the parties, the borrower and the syndicate, to avoid their respective obligations; the consequences of such acts would be obvious.

Where however a syndicated loan agreement will not be governed by English law, the situation may be different, and rather unpredictable. Alternatively, the parties in the event of maintaining a departure from performing contractual obligations can always refer their dispute to an arbitral tribunal, but they may like to bear in mind that the recognition and enforcement of an arbitral award might present another problem, requiring the parties to expend money on arbitration proceedings.

[26] [1956] AC 696 at 729.
[27] [1918] AC 119 at 139.
[28] [1962] AC 93.
[29] [1983] 1 WLR 1469.
[30] [1983] 2 Lloyd's Rep 579; see also Schmitthoff's *The Law and Practice of International Trade*, Carole Murray, D Holloway et al. (eds), London, Sweet & Maxwell (latest edition), the chapter on Frustration of Contracts.

Based on the above discussion, it may be maintained that in the event of any differences arising under the loan agreement, the best means of settling them would be to negotiate their differences, and if that should fail, then they should refer their dispute to conciliation which should not entail considerable costs.

7.6.5 *Hardship Clause*

A "hardship" clause is different from a *force majeure* clause. The basis of a *force majeure* has already been discussed. It simply stands for a situation which could not be foreseen by any prudent businessman, but it has now the force of avoiding a contract which was concluded in "good faith." It is for the courts to determine how real was the *force majeure* situation. It must be an obstacle which may not have been foreseen, but it is proved to be the cause of frustrating the contract. One of the most recent examples of hardship to businesses leading to frustration would be the pandemic which is known as COVID-19 (Coronavirus Disease 2019) which has compelled many business houses in the world to temporarily close down, if not permanently.

Many business houses, even some of the large ones in the UK, have been experiencing "hardship" in settling their contract-based debts. In its attempt to minimise the effect of financial adversity the British Treasury has already provided for a number of financial aids to come to the rescue of the business houses. The governmental instruction for an almost total "lockdown" has prevented them from opening their businesses for over a year, and this hardship has to be appreciated by everybody in the British society. The lending banks, in particular, are required to appreciate that they would not receive any re-payments of the debts attracted by these business houses for some time. Whereas a *force majeure* situation, if accepted by the courts, will excuse the performance of the contract, a "hardship" situation will, on the other hand, simply defer the performance of the lending-borrowing contract. The International Chamber of Commerce (ICC in Paris) has also recognised the effect of hardship on the business world. In view of the example cited above, it is strongly recommended that a "hardship clause" be incorporated into a syndicated loan agreement. The ICC Hardship Clause is recommended as an informative document, but no one is allowed to copy any of its provisions; and no discussion of it is needed here.

7.6.6 Market Volatility

The world market seems to be closely linked to US dollars, mainly for historical reasons. But US dollar is a very volatile currency in consequence of which the markets of investments, shares, stocks and other financial instruments become volatile; the result of a volatile market is clear—no investor of any financial product can precisely predict how investments in various instruments will perform. The risk of any financial market volatility is a constant risk, but can any effective protection be taken against this risk?

In order to ensure that borrowers from syndications are not victims of such market volatility, they should, in a separate clause in the syndication agreement, provide for a fixed rate of interest in the loan agreement, although it may not take away the risk entirely, simply because the currency in which loans and prices are expressed is a volatile currency. Both borrowers and lenders are now required to review this practice.

7.6.7 Change of Borrowers and/or Lenders

If the duration of the loan is rather long, the possibility of changing the corporate structure of the borrower may not be overruled; the same possibility should be anticipated of the lenders too. Thus, a clause in the loan agreement should be incorporated to provide for succession of the new borrowers with the same conditions, and in the event of the lenders changing their corporate structures, the same procedure should be followed without changing the lending and borrowing conditions, as changing the terms and conditions of the loan will amount to a breach of the loan agreement. As stated earlier that in drafting a loan agreement, all possibilities of its future volatility, that is, until all the money have been paid off, have to be considered seriously and the relevant clauses incorporated accordingly.

7.6.8 Exclusion of Any Subsequent Legislation

Ideally, a syndicated loan agreement should clearly provide that the current agreement shall not be affected in any way by any subsequent legislation, as usually, no legislation is enacted with retroactive effect. Of course, in the event of a regime change this situation may be even more unpredictable. Alternatively, the new regime might instruct its central bank to make all loan agreements, including syndicated loan agreements, to be subject to the new regulations or governmental legislation, as a sovereign entity, but it will make the new regime extremely unpopular. Nevertheless, it is just a distant possibility.

7.6.9 Performance-Related Loans

Borrowers initially may be objecting to this kind of condition to a loan, but in reality, it is in the interests of the borrowers to have this kind of condition, as such a condition help them to pay back the loan on time, or even before the stipulated date. What they are supposed to seriously consider is whether the performance level is too onerous for them, and in that event, they should object to the condition and negotiate conditions which would be achievable for them. Usually, performance levels are progressive in nature. If a loan is paid off by the stipulated date or even earlier than the final date, the borrowers' prospects of getting another loan in the future become higher.

7.6.10 Confidentiality

All information relating to the borrower(s) including their financial documents and the Facility letter, which is usually issued by the lender(s), deserves confidentiality. In fact, both borrower(s) and lender(s) are required to sign a confidentiality agreement in the form which may be agreed to by both the parties.

In the event of the current lenders being changed for whatever reasons, a similar confidentiality agreement should be drafted in the form which may be agreed to by both the parties, unless of course, new lenders are prepared to accept the contents of the former confidentiality agreement, but they will still be required to make a fresh agreement which must be signed by both the parties, preferably in the presence of two witnesses.

7.6.11 Financial Indebtedness of the Borrower(s)

The borrowers are usually required to disclose their indebtedness, if any, in the way the lenders would like to see them, for instance:

(1) the amount of money borrowed including any form of interest on that money;

(2) any credit facility obtained by the borrowers including documentary credit facilities, note purchase and so on;
(3) any balance outstanding under any financial lease;
(4) money raised by selling or assigning any financial assets on terms which would entail recourse to the borrowers in the event of non-payment of financial assets when due;
(5) any counter-guarantee provided by the borrowers in respect of any bond or guarantee or stand-by letter of credit or any other instrument which has been issued by a third party which might entail a demand on the borrowers;
(6) any derivative transaction which has been entered into in connection with protection against any fluctuation in any price; and
(7) any guarantee or counter indemnity against financial loss that the borrowers gave for any other debts.

The caution must be entered that this list of liabilities may not be a complete one which a borrower may have incurred. The extent and the nature of liability in certain cases may be different. Thus, a disclosure declaration from a borrower would be a safe document to be obtained by the prospective lenders.

7.6.12 Material Adverse Effect

It is to be emphasised that in respect of any loan agreement, whether syndicated or not, the lender(s) will hold the upper hand. This clause would simply mean that the lender has the privilege of taking the view that any event or circumstance is likely to materially and adversely affect the borrower's ability to perform or comply with all or any of its obligations, or is likely to materially and adversely affect the business or is likely to result in a finance document not being valid and therefore unenforceable or in respect of a Debenture, the borrower failed to provide the lender appropriate security over the assets which were supposed to be subject to security under the Debenture.

7.6.13 Admissible Security

The admissibility or inadmissibility of a security to be offered by a borrower is an issue over which the lender's decision must prevail.

7.6.14 *Qualified Lenders*

The lender's appointment is determined by referring to the provisions of the relevant legislation in the UK.

7.6.15 *An Interpretation Clause and Certain Other Clauses*

This is a standard clause which is incorporated into the loan agreement.

A *Condition Precedent Clause* by virtue of which the lender(s) would request the borrower(s) to satisfy certain conditions precedent prior to their allowing the borrower(s) any drawdown right.

A *Drawdown Request Clause* is meant for the borrower(s)—prior to their drawing any money they will be required to complete a drawdown request form or document.

An Interest Clause and the Duration of the Interest Period

This is self-explanatory. The question remains whether the rate of interest would be fixed or flexible.

7.6.16 *Business Days/Non-business Days*

This is self-explanatory and is governed by the calendar of the market to which the loan relates.

7.6.17 *Voluntary Pre-payment and Repayment of Loans*

7.6.17.1 Default Interest

This is a clause which is very essential for the lenders for obvious reasons. It may be payable on demand too.

7.6.17.2 Voluntary Cancellation

Change of control on the part of the borrower(s). In the event of occasioning a change of control within its corporate entity, the borrower(s) will have an obligation to notify the lenders as soon as possible. But the lenders have the right either to accept or reject the control system. In the event of the lenders rejecting the new control structure within the borrower's corporate structure, the lenders will have the right to cancel their commitment and declare the remaining part of the unpaid loan outstanding and payable with accrued interest.

7.6.18 Tax and Tax Deduction, Tax Credits, Stamp Duty and Value-Added Tax

Indemnities. Under this clause the lender(s) will specify the grounds on which the borrower(s) will be required to indemnify the former, and the currency in which the borrower(s) will be required to indemnify the lender(s) by the time that may be stipulated by the lender(s). Each indemnity is a separate and independent obligation from the borrower's other obligations that may be stipulated in the loan agreement. The lenders can incorporate a variety of indemnities in the loan agreement, and it seems that the borrowers may have very little room for bargaining on this issue.

7.6.19 Mitigation by the Lender(s)

In certain special circumstances the lender(s) might be prepared to mitigate or even remove certain conditions in consultation with the borrower(s), including transferring the facility to another office or financial institution. The decision whether a mitigating circumstance exists or not or whether the borrower(s) should be allowed any mitigating circumstance is a matter entirely for the lenders to consider.

7.6.20 Negative Pledge

Under this clause, the borrower is required to promise certain things it should not do, for example:

- not to create any security over any of its assets;
- not to sell, transfer or dispose of any of its receivables on recourse terms;
- enter into any preferential arrangement which will have a similar effect.

It is for the lenders to identify these "negative pledges" which would be applicable to borrowers.

7.6.21 Events of Default

The events usually include the following: non-payment; non-compliance with any provision of the financial documents. The lenders may allow a period of time to correct these defaults.

7.6.22 Cross-Default

It is comparable to a double-default; the borrowers must bear in mind that in any lending process, the lenders hold upper hands.

7.6.23 Insolvency

This applies to borrowers; a reasonable ground for lenders to stop paying any part of the outstanding amount; instead, the lenders will usually be regarded as the preferred creditors, perhaps after the inland revenue authorities.

7.6.24 Lender(s)' Right to Change, Assign or Create Security Over Rights

Need not be explained; provisions of this clause in loan agreement are usually clearly stated.

7.6.24.1 The Lender(s)' Right to Disclose Confidential Information
This is usually a very lengthy clause, and the borrowers have very little or perhaps no right at all to oppose any of the provisions of this clause.

7.6.24.2 Lender(s)' Right to Set-off
Under this clause, the lender may at any time set off any liability of the borrower to the lender against any liability of the lender to the borrower.

There does not exist any obligation for a lender to exercise this right under the clause entitled set-off; however, in the event of the lender exercising the right to set off the borrower must be promptly notified.

7.6.25 Third-Party Rights

A third party to a syndicated loan, concluded under the relevant English law, has no right under the Contracts (Rights of Third Parties) Act 1999 to enjoy or enforce the benefit of any term of this agreement, although his/its other rights would remain intact which may be available to him/it under other relevant legislation.

7.6.26 *Know Your Customer*

This is a local market practice. If the lender is obliged to comply with the above-mentioned or any similar precedent, it is the borrower's obligation to supply this information promptly to the lenders upon their request for it.

7.7 The Issue of Jurisdiction and the Governing Law of a Syndicated Loan Agreement

The Law of Contract in England and Wales clearly suggests that the place of contracting (jurisdiction) provides the governing law. Thus, if a syndicated loan agreement is concluded in England and Wales, it is natural that the agreement would be governed by the Law of England and Wales.

7.8 Conclusions

The primary purpose of this chapter is to familiarise the readers with some of the complex aspects of a syndicated loan agreement. It has to be admitted that in agreements of this type there is hardly any room for negotiation between a borrower and a lender, as the latter will always hold the upper hand. The borrowers may only draw the attention of the lender(s) if they are not familiar with some of the relevant legislation in England and Wales.

This chapter also listed the most important clauses that are usually incorporated into a syndicated loan agreement, in addition to providing a rather brief interpretation of those clauses as they will be automatically incorporated into a standard loan agreement. Certain other standard clauses are also incorporated into these agreements.

Finally, under the current practice the borrowers have hardly any room for negotiation of the terms and conditions of these agreements, from this point of view these agreements are very much one-sided instruments.

CHAPTER 8

The United Nations System and Diplomacy

8.1 Introduction

The world is changing in all senses of the term and will keep changing; if one accepts this progress, then eventually one would be required to rapidly devise ways and means of tackling these changes in a way which would benefit the entire international community. In order to be able to tackle the challenges, diplomats are required to be dynamic and constant learners. The general view of the international community seems to be to condemn the United Nations by maintaining that it is a useless organisation without realising that if that is true then it is the international community, including the diplomatic community, that are to be blamed for it, but it is hastened to add that based on the author's experience not all diplomats are so.

A nonchalant attitude in regard to the UN has become evident; but a truly international organisation is needed to resolve international problems unless an alternative platform is formed which might also be subject to criticism. The international community including the diplomatic community should have much more sophisticated training especially in the form of negotiating techniques, and conciliatory measures, rather than being engaged in warfares, which unfortunately seems to have become the contemporary norm.

This is not to suggest that the diplomats in the contemporary world are not competent enough to resolve the issues in the current climate;

C. Chatterjee, *Negotiating Techniques in Diplomacy and Business Contracts*, https://doi.org/10.1007/978-3-030-81732-9_8

what is suggested however that more dynamism, with understanding of the new types of problems often contributed to by technology or new type of power politics to which often the poor States become victims, should now receive much more attention of the entire international community than ever before. Furthermore, certain other issues such as slavery and slave trade, discrimination between people based on race, culture or origin, sexual exploitation, breach of fundamental rights, environmental damage, cybercrime and espionage have become so rampant that these now may not be effectively tackled by one or a few States; rather, in order to eradicate such practices a united front on a universal platform would be essential. Abuse of technology seems to be at the root of many of these crimes.

The country leaders, despite their areas of differences for whatever reasons, should now make their best efforts to join their hands together to iron out those differences and discuss and settle issues at the UN platform. However unpalatable it might sound, the fact of the matter is that not all diplomats are as familiar with the UN system as they should be; furthermore, given the problem-ridden world we live in, the diplomats are now required to comprehend the complexity of the problems and issues from a truly inter-State process and in a friendly manner.

There is no need to glamorise warfares; the entire world knows the miseries warfares bring to people, and yet, many of the leaders of the world community do not seem to have learned the adverse effect of warfares. They return to the olden days of history when warfares were a common phenomenon to establish the heroism and superiority of the nation and gradually the State.[1] Furthermore, in choosing diplomats many countries are failing to determine the inner qualities of their chosen people to see whether they would be able to effectively interact with their colleagues and try to settle all differences between themselves through negotiations and/or by conciliatory measures. Indeed, the UN Charter has also provided for these means among others to settle their differences. Article 33 of the UN Charter, which has been quoted in this chapter, has identified the means that diplomats should adopt in settling domestic disputes between factions, if any, as well as inter-State disputes.

[1] See, for example, Niall Ferguson, op. cit.

8.2 The Qualities Required of Modern-Day Diplomats

In Chap. 2 of this book the qualities that a diplomat should ideally possess have been identified; the days of employer and the employees (the diplomats in this context) relationship should be reviewed. Although diplomats are the representatives of their respective States, their mandates should contain a degree of flexibility, as nobody may know in advance what kind of outcome both the parties might reach through negotiations on settling an issue or a matter.

Modern-day diplomats must be even more articulate than ever before. In whichever UN language he/she may have decided to speak, he/she must be articulate and demonstrate clearly his/her understanding of the issue or the matter at a UN platform, including those of its Specialised Agencies. Diplomats must not be guided by any superiority-inferiority complex. They must also be patient and tolerant people to listen to their colleagues at a UN platform.

All issues which may lead to warfares, in particular, should be referred to the appropriate organ of the UN. All issues or matters which might adversely affect State(s) such as earthquakes, floods, epidemics or pandemics, cybercrimes to name but a few must be discussed at a UN forum to reach a consensus, whether in the form of a Declaration or a Resolution or a Convention and influence universally rather than maintaining the strange view that they are not binding.

The UN is not a sovereign entity; it is merely a "club" so to say of the sovereign States, and these States have undertaken the obligations to implement the directions that may be rendered by it, and these directions may be issued in different forms: Conventions, Declarations, Resolutions, Recommendations, Charters and so on.

8.3 A Brief Discussion of the Guidelines Offered by the United Nations and the Diplomats' Role

8.3.1 Declarations

According to O'Connell, States can issue declarations on certain matters either jointly or even unilaterally. The question whether they give rise to any binding obligations or not " depends upon whether they can be read in a context of consensus."[2] He then, in support of his aforesaid opinion, referred to the *Austro-German Customs Regime* case[3] in which the Permanent Court of International Justice stated that the Protocol which was signed in Geneva on 4 October 1922 by Austria, Czechoslovakia, France, Great Britain, Italy and subsequently acceded to by Belgium and Spain included the following:

> ... it cannot be denied that although it took the form of a declaration, Austria did assume thereby certain undertakings in the economic sphere ... it is well known that such engagements may be taken in the form of treaties, conventions, declarations, agreements, protocols or exchange of notes.[4]

The truth of the matter is that the intention of the parties often determines the binding nature of a declaration; however, the "intention" must be determined by ascertaining whether in the process of determining an intention a good mixture of developed and developing States gave their consent to be bound by it or not. The difficulties in ascertaining this intention received the attention of the International Court of Justice (ICJ) in the *Ambatielos* claim.[5]

Sometime in July 1919, Ambatielos, a Greek Shipowner, negotiated with the UK Shipping Controller a contract for the purchase of nine steamships which would be built in Hong Kong and Shanghai at a price of £2,750,000. The contract was negotiated in London by a Greek minister along with a brother of Ambatielos. The contract incorporated a clause as to the delivery of the vessels in accordance with the terms and manner agreed upon by the parties, and within the time agreed. But the government of the UK denied that any delivery date had been agreed upon. The Greek government maintained that the dates of delivery of the steamers were written on a separate piece of paper which was recorded in the ministry's records. Whereas the Greek government maintained that the delivery date was an integral part of the contract, the government of the UK maintained, on the other hand, that those dates were merely an indication when the delivery was likely to take place. But, nevertheless, the Greek government rigidly maintained that the suppliers of the steamers knew the

[2] D P O'Connell, *International Law*, Vol.1, London, Stevens (1970) at 198.

[3] PCIJ, Series A/B No.41 (1931) at 47.

[4] Ibid.

[5] Preliminary Objections, *ICJ Reports* (1952) at 28 and at 40 et seq.; see also 23 *International Law Reports* at 306.

dates of delivery. The vessels were delivered later than the alleged delivery dates.

Without going into the other details as to the additional payment made by the Greek government, it should be stated that this was eventually referred to an arbitration tribunal. The Board of Trade, as successors to the Ministry of Shipping, brought an action on mortgaged deeds executed by Ambatielos, who put his claims forward by way of defence, instead of proceeding with the arbitration. Hill J rendered his judgement in favour of the UK government for possession and sale of certain vessels which had been delivered, and the principal and interest thereon under the mortgages. The UK government declined to produce certain inter-departmental minutes under the English law of procedure which, according to the Greek government, amounted to an abuse of Crown privilege and a denial of justice. Ambatielos appealed and sought leave from the Court of Appeal to call witnesses, including Major Laing, but that was refused. Ambatielos did not refer this matter to the House of Lords.

It is important to point out that this matter was referred to a diplomatic level in 1925, but eventually it came before the International Court of Justice in 1952. The ICJ found that it lacked jurisdiction to decide the case on its merits, but it was competent to decide whether the UK government was under an obligation under the Declaration made at the time of signing the Anglo-Greek Treaty of Commerce and Navigation of 1926 to submit the matter to arbitration in so far as the claim was based on the Treaty of Commerce and Navigation, 1886. The Court held that the UK government was under an obligation to submit Ambatielos' claim to arbitration under the 1886 Treaty.

Although a rather complex case, it at least confirms the binding nature of a Declaration, irrespective of its age. A Declaration shall certainly be construed as a binding promise if it is actually implemented by States. Such is the legal position of the 1960 Declaration on the Independence of Colonial Peoples which have already been discussed in this work. The Rio Declaration of 1992, although predominantly a document developed by the developing countries, private foreign investors should take it seriously.

As to the other forms of instruments that are usually adopted by the UN, the situation is rather complex. At the root of this problem, lies the genuineness of the desires of the participants. As regards Declarations, it is settled, by virtue of the decisions of the World Court in the *Austro-German Customs Regime* case and the *Ambatielos* case, that it is the quality of the "intention" of the parties concerned which is easily determinable in regard to rather philosophically charged topics, with a socio-economic dimension to it—the 1960 Declaration and the 1992 Rio Declaration; a high level of public awareness of the issue(s) would be a helpful factor too.

As regards other instruments which usually are named as Resolutions, Charters, Conventions, Recommendations and Treaties, without maintaining any order of priority which, in fact, does not exist in so naming them, it may be observed that the force of emotion may also be found in Chapter XI of the UN Charter entitled "Declaration regarding non-self-governing territories" too.

Article 73—The opening paragraph of this Article should affirm the above-mentioned view:

> Members of the United Nations which have or assume responsibilities for the administration of territories whose peoples have not yet attained a full measure of self-government recognise the principle that the interests of the inhabitants of these territories are paramount, and accept as a sacred trust the obligation to promote to the utmost, within the system of international peace and security established by the present Charter, the well-being of the inhabitants of these territories ….

By the same token, Article 74 provided that:

> Members of the United Nations also agree that their policy in respect of the territories to which this Chapter[6] applies, no less than in respect of their metropolitan areas, must be based on the general principle of good neighbourliness, due account being taken of the interests and well-being of the rest of the world, in social, economic and commercial matters.

The validity of the Declaration may not be questioned in view of what has been stated above.

Treaties, be they bilateral or multilateral, are binding on the parties which legally accepted them. Treaties are currently governed by the Vienna Convention on the Law of Treaties 1969. Regrettably, although the UN Charter is a multilateral treaty, many of its provisions are most honoured in their breach, and one of the purposes of writing this chapter is to ascertain the reasons thereof.

[6] Chapter XI of the UN Charter.

Many of the parties to the UN Charter which formally undertook to follow the obligations under it unfortunately tend to disregard them. The Charter of Economic Rights and Duties of States 1974, which contains very many good and instructive provisions, failed. This Charter provided abolition of apartheid[7] and commodity cartels[8] among other criticism-provoking provisions. There was no reason why the proposal for the abolition of apartheid was not accepted by all. Nevertheless, this Charter has some very good and important issues on which the international community may like to work. This document identified some of the important socio-economic issues about five decades ago, which have come true. One may like to look up Chapter III of this Charter entitled Common Responsibilities Towards the International Community. Article 29, for example, provided, inter alia, that:

> The sea-bed and ocean floor and the subsoil thereof, beyond the limits of national jurisdiction, as well as the resources of the area, are the common heritage of mankind. On the basis of the principles adopted by the General Assembly in Resolution 2749 (XXV) of 17 December 1970, all States shall ensure that the exploration of the area and exploitation of its resources are carried out exclusively for peaceful purposes and that the benefits derived therefrom are shared equitably by all States ....

Article 30 of the same Charter provided, inter alia, that:

> The protection, preservation and enhancement of the environment for the present and future generations is the responsibility of all States. All States shall endeavour to establish their own environmental and developmental policies in conformity with such responsibility ....[9]

As regards "resolutions" of the UN General Assembly, one should not go by the number of the Member States of the UN which voted for them, one is required to see the voting structure, that is, the ratio of votes between the developed and developing States.

[7] Article 16.

[8] Article 6.

[9] See also S K Chatterjee, "The Charter of Economic Rights and Duties of States: An Evaluation after Fifteen Years", *International and Comparative Law Quarterly* (1991).

8.3.2 Recommendations

According to the Oxford Dictionary of English,[10] "Recommendation" means:

> ... a suggestion or proposal as to the best course of action, especially one put forward by an authoritative body.

All States may find recommendations of the General Assembly or any other organ of the UN worth following; indeed, recommendations may have a binding force too.[11] There is no doubt that the United Nations and one of its principal organ, the General Assembly, are both authoritative bodies in the world. Unfortunately, very little attention seems to have been paid to the UN by most of the countries which are engaged in warfares particularly on the grounds that the UN General Assembly's resolutions or recommendations are not binding. In other words, they fail to pay any attention to the authentic meaning of the term "Recommendation." In this connection it may also be maintained that many of the members of the United Nations, in particular, many of the developing States, along with some of the established rich States are in clear violation of Articles 1 and 2 (Purposes and Principles of the UN). Each paragraph of Article 2 represents a binding obligation for each of the Member States of the Organisation but many of them are in breach of these binding obligations.

There exists evidence that some of the recommendations/declarations adopted by the UN General Assembly have legally binding effect. Take, for example, the Declaration on the Granting of Independence to Colonial Countries and Peoples, 1960. This was a UN General Assembly Resolution.[12] In adopting this resolution 89 States voted for it, and the following countries abstained: Australia, Belgium, Dominican Republic, France, Portugal, Spain, Union of South Africa, the UK and the US. Strangely enough, although it was primarily a UN General Assembly Resolution, no country raised any issue against it on whether it was a legally binding resolution; most of the former colonies accepted it without raising any question about its binding effect. Indeed, it met with the contemporary aspirations of the former colonies. The UN General Assembly also upgraded its status by calling it a Declaration.

[10] *Oxford Dictionary of English*, Oxford, Oxford University Press (2010) at 1484.

[11] See F B Sloan, "The Binding Force of a 'Recommendation' of the General Assembly of the UN" 25 *British Year Book of International Law* (1948) 1.

[12] Resolution 1514 (XV) of 14 December 1960.

In the Preamble to this Resolution/Declaration, it was stated, inter alia, that:

> Recognizing the passionate yearning[13] for freedom in all dependent peoples and the decisive role of such peoples in the attainment of their independence.

It went on to state that:

> Recognizing that the peoples of the world ardently desire the end of colonisation in all its manifestations.

The peoples' desire to end colonisation was also taken into consideration in adopting this Resolution/Declaration. This Declaration clearly indicates that it is for people to emphasise their desire to achieve something which should be brought to the attention of the UN General Assembly rather than maintain an unfounded belief that the UN General Assembly exists merely as an institution of the UN.

The text of this Declaration further confirmed, inter alia, that:

Paragraph 2 All peoples have the right to self-determination by virtue of that right they freely determine their political status and freely pursue their economic, social and cultural development.

Paragraph 3 Inadequacy of political, economic, social or educational preparedness should never serve as a pretext for delaying independence.

This kind of encouraging message may originate at the UN level provided of course the people show their solidarity and aspiration for the improvement of their socio-economic progress, including investment, education and so on.

Without any socio-economic freedom (emancipation), political independence of people would be meaningless. In an attempt to materialise the above, it is assumed that the UN General Assembly adopted in 1962 the Resolution on Permanent Sovereignty over Natural Resources. Full exercise of sovereignty over a country's natural resources should allow them to enjoy the benefits of the country's natural resources.

[13] Emphasis added.

However, this Resolution supplements the 1960 Resolution, but it fails to highlight the importance of developing human resources in the country, capacity-building, although this has been identified by paragraph 6 of the Declaration perhaps only peripherally. Paragraph 6 of the Declaration provides that:

> International co-operation for the economic development of developing countries, whether in the form of public or private capital investments, exchange of goods and services, technical assistance, or exchange of scientific information, shall be such as to further their independent national development and shall be based upon respect for their sovereignty over their natural wealth and reserves.

What was entirely true in 1962 may not remain so in all respects in the twenty-first century. Technical assistance from foreign sources proves to be essential, but how the terms and conditions of such assistance are determined by the providers of technical assistance or exchange of scientific information and the recipients of them matters. These deals are usually struck between two public entities. In order to lessen the dependency of the developing countries upon the developed ones, the developing countries should negotiate with the providers of technical assistance. The nature of such assistance should be training for the indigenous people in order to ensure that in a certain short period of time the recipient country fully attains expertise and the need for technical assistance minimises. But unfortunately, this has not been achieved as yet by the majority of the developing countries. Thus, based on these Resolutions, developing countries, where necessary, should pay attention to such important issues in order to strengthen their position as trading partners.

Finally, one should also in this context refer to the UN General Assembly Resolution 3281(XXIX) entitled The Charter of Economic Rights and Duties of States of 1974. This Charter has provided the international community with the Fundamentals of International Economic Relations, in addition to the Economic Rights and Duties of States, and the Common Responsibilities towards the International Community.[14]

The above three examples would be enough to establish that there does not yet exist any unanimity among the Member States of the United Nations on the special characteristics of each of these three instruments:

[14] See further S K Chatterjee, op. cit.,

recommendations, Declarations and Resolutions. But would a "label" to the instrument make any difference? Take, for example, the 1960 Declaration on the Granting of Independence to Colonial Countries and Peoples—whether it was a Declaration or a Resolution or even a recommendation it would not have made any difference in its effect. It was not only a timely Resolution/Declaration by the UN General Assembly, but also more importantly, fully supported the aspirations of the colonised people; it would not have mattered what title the members of the UN would have expected as the legal distinction between them seems to be minimal.[15] It is the intention to be bound that is what matters. The dictionary meaning of the term "recommendations" has already been identified.

The Oxford Dictionary of English defined the term "Declaration" as:

> a formal or explicit statement or announcement or written public announcement of intention or of the terms of an agreement.[16]

A Resolution, on the other hand, has been defined by the same dictionary in the following way:

> … a firm decision to do or not to do something … a formal expression of opinion or intention agreed on by a legislative body or other formal meeting.[17]

Thus, what are the basic differences between these expressions? The 1960 and 1962 Declaration/Resolution received the support of the majority of the Member States of the UN simply because these resolutions/declarations timely met the aspirations of the very high majority of the existing members of the UN.

Incidentally, the Member States of the UN missed a golden opportunity by not following in full the Charter of Economic Rights and Duties of States. Of course, many of the developed States disliked the issue of "apartheid" and racial discrimination mentioned in Article 16 of the Charter, as they genuinely declined to accept the provisions of paragraph (c) of Article 2 of the Charter. It is now part of customary international

[15] See also F B Sloan, "The Binding Force of a Recommendation of the General Assembly of the United Nations" 29 *British Year Book of International Law* (1948), 14.

[16] Op. cit., at 453–454.

[17] Op. cit., at 1512.

law which clearly states that in the event of "taking" of any kind of foreign assets, compensation must be paid in accordance with the market value of the asset. But regrettably apartheid still exists.

One of the principal objectives of the Charter was to draw the attention of the Member States to what they were supposed to fulfil to achieve economic freedom and democracy in addition to gaining grounds in transnational trade and investment.

8.3.3 Treaties

Treaties establishing customary rules of international law bind third parties too. The case which should be exemplified on this issue would be the *Nuclear Tests Cases*, 1974,[18] in which France was carrying on nuclear tests, allegedly for peaceful purposes in the Pacific. France was not a party to the Nuclear Test Ban Treaty. Australia and New Zealand brought an action against France, and the latter initially pleaded the *res inter alios acta* doctrine before the International Court of Justice, to which the Court stated that a treaty which has established a customary rule of international law will bind every State, irrespective of whether it is a party to the Treaty or not. Of course, the government of France eventually withdrew its defence in that case.

The legal status of many of the international conventions still remains unsettled. If a State has openly accepted, including where its parliamentary ratification is necessary (unless a State does not require to follow any ratification procedure), whereby international conventions will automatically come into force, then that convention may be treated as binding for the State, and even for a contesting State in a judicial dispute provided the latter State has also accepted it. Examples of binding international conventions (i.e. they bind all recognised States) would be:

(a) The Vienna Convention on Diplomatic Relations, 1961
(b) The Vienna Convention on Consular Relations, 1963
(c) The Vienna Convention on the Law of Treaties, 1969
(d) The Law of the Sea Convention, 1982

[18] *ICJ Reports*, 1974; 57 ILR pp. 398, 412

In this context, it would be opportune to reproduce Article 38 of the Statute of the International Court of Justice, which also indicates the legally binding effect of some of the instruments discussed in this chapter. It provides that:

1. The Court, whose function is to decide in accordance with international law such disputes as are submitted to it, shall apply:
   - (a) international conventions, whether general or particular, establishing rules expressly recognised by the contesting States;
   - (b) international custom, as evidence of a general practice accepted as law;
   - (c) the general principles of law recognised by civilised nations;
   - (d) subject to the provisions of Article 59, judicial decisions and the teachings of the most highly qualified publicists of the various nations, as subsidiary means for the determination of the rules of law.
2. This provision shall not prejudice the power of the Court to decide a case *ex aequo et bono*,[19] if the parties agree thereto.[20]

In sum, in this constantly changing world, which tends to create even more uncertainties for peoples' lives, combined with constant warfares in different parts of the world causing immeasurable human miseries, environmental damages, unnecessary deaths and so on, which is almost a never-ending list of miseries initiated and caused by human beings, and yet no positive action is being taken by anybody let alone diplomats. Apparently, based on the miseries caused, it may be deduced that the diplomatic world seem to have lost faith in the United Nations, as well as in effective negotiations between and among (if necessary) relevant parties. Article 33 of the UN Charter provides that:

1. The parties to any dispute, the continuance of which is likely to endanger the maintenance of international peace and security, shall, first of all, seek a solution by negotiation, enquiry, mediation, conciliation,

[19] It means that the court can exercise its power to decide a case by applying the principles of equity.

[20] Article 59 of the Statute of the ICJ: "The decision of the Court has no binding force except between the parties and in respect of that particular case."

arbitration, judicial settlement, resort to regional agencies or arrangements, or other peaceful means of their own choice.
2. The Security Council shall, when it deems necessary, call upon the parties to settle their dispute by such means.

This has been the basic theme of this work. Contemporary diplomats should have special training in settling disputes, inter-State or domestic, by peaceful means (paragraph 1 of Article 33), and if that should fail, they should refer the dispute to the Security Council. Of all the peaceful means of settling disputes, Article 33, paragraph 1, recommended that it is emphasised that diplomats should really have a very good command in the negotiating techniques bearing in mind that we now live in an entirely different and changing world. But the contemporary world seems to be going backwards to reach the days of warfares. The predecessors of the United Nations, the League of Nations, failed the international community in abolishing warfares, and strengthening the peaceful means of settling disputes. Article 15 paragraph 7 of the League Covenant provided that:

> If the Council fails to reach a report which is unanimously agreed to by the members thereof, other than the Representatives of one or more of the parties to the dispute, the Members of the League reserve to themselves the right to take such action as they shall consider necessary for the maintenance of right and justice.

The above provision is self-explanatory.[21]

In order to abolish warfares and to bring peace in the world on a permanent basis and also for the recognition of the rights of all people irrespective of their origins to self-determination in addition to promoting socio-economic development in the world, in particular, in the developing world, the United Nations was set up on 24 October 1945.[22]

Governmental and diplomatic activities should be directed at the issues identified by the UN Charter as to why the contemporary diplomats are required to be extremely familiar with the current political activities, which are often based on sophisticated technologies. It has been decided to

[21] Interested readers may like to consult F P Walters, *A History of the League of Nations*, London, Oxford University Press (1952) and subsequent reprints, a very instructive work on the history of the League of Nations.

[22] See the Preamble to the UN Charter.

briefly analyse the structures and functions of the UN and its most important Specialised Agencies and other offices under it, which diplomats may find useful.

8.3.4 *Resolutions*

According to the Oxford Dictionary of English, a Resolution means:

> A firm decision to do or not to do something.
>
> A formal expression of opinion or intention agreed on by a legislative body or other formal meeting, typically after taking a vote.[23]

There does not exist any clear-cut answer as to when a resolution, whether it is adopted by the UN General Assembly or the Security Council, might be binding. Indeed, the term "resolution" does not appear in the text of the Charter. Take for example UN General Assembly Resolution of 1962 (1803(XVIII)) entitled Permanent Sovereignty over Natural Resources addressed to foreign investors is treated as a binding resolution. Similarly, a Declaration adopted by the UN General Assembly on 14 December 1960 (also described as a Resolution No. 1514(XV)) entitled Granting of Independence to the Colonial Countries and Peoples is treated as a binding resolution. On the other hand, most experts consider majority of the UN General Assembly Resolutions to be non-binding. It is important to mention that Articles 10 and 14 of the UN Charter refer to the UN General Assembly Resolutions as "recommendations." Nevertheless, General Assembly Resolutions on budgetary matters is clearly binding on its Member States.

The UN Charter authorises the Security Council to take action and measures (the latter to be confirmed by the Security Council too) on behalf of the members of the UN to make decisions and recommendations. The members of the UN have allowed the Organisation the required legal authority, and they also agreed to give the UN every assistance in any action taken in accordance with the Charter. Under Article 25 the "Members of the UN agreed to accept and carry out the decisions of the Security Council in accordance with the present Charter." Security Council has also the authority to take measures under Chapter VI of it and it can

[23] Op. cit., at 1512.

take appropriate action under Chapter VII of the Charter (enforcement action) for the maintenance of international peace and security.

The Charter has also empowered the Security Council to take appropriate measures and action under Articles 41 and 42 of it. At the time of accepting the UN Charter, the Member States of the UN authorised the Security Council to take measures and actions, as and when necessary, in order to maintain international peace and security, and the Member States are required to cooperate with the Security Council on this issue. Whether the Security Council's measures (under Chapter VI) or action (under Chapter VII) are based on decisions or recommendations rather than resolutions is simply an academic issue. The most important issue is that the Security Council's members, both permanent and rotating, have decided to take these measures and actions, and that the Member States of the Organisation are in such situations required to cooperate with it in the way it may direct them. This requirement must be satisfied—it is legally binding.

8.4 A Brief Analysis of the Structures, Objectives and Functions of the United Nations and Its Specialised Agencies, and Other Important Offices

There is little point in going into the historical background of the United Nations in the context of this work. It is important however to mention that the UN was set up soon after the Second World War ended in 1945.[24]

At the outset, it would be apposite to remind diplomats of the obligations their respective States by virtue of them being a member of the

[24] In relation to the history and early growth of the UN, see Goodrich and Hambro, *Charter of the UN*, London, Stevens & Sons, published under the auspices of The London Institute of World Affairs (1949); H Kelsen, *Law of the UN*, London, Stevens (1950); S S Goodspeed, *The Nature and Function of International Organization*, New York, Oxford University Press (1959); H G Nicholas, *The United Nations as a Political Institution*, Oxford, Oxford University Press (1952); H V Evatt, *The UN*, Oxford University Press (1948); N Bentwich and A Martin, *A Commentary on the Charter of the United Nations*, London, Macmillan (1951); R Higgins, *The Development of International Law Through the Political Organs of the United Nations*, Oxford, Oxford University Press, issued under the auspices of the Royal Institute of International Affairs (1963); M Shaw, *International Law*, Cambridge, Cambridge University Press (latest edition); Bowett's *Law of International Institutions*, P Sands and P Klein (eds), London, Sweet & Maxwell (latest edition).

United Nations were determined to perform. The Preamble to the UN Charter provided that:

> We the Peoples of the United Nations Determined to save succeeding generations from the scourge of war, which twice in our lifetime has brought untold sorrow to mankind, and
>
> to reaffirm faith in fundamental human rights, in the dignity and worth of the human person, in the equal rights of men and women and nations large and small, and
>
> to establish conditions under which justice and respect for the obligations arising from treaties and other sources of international law can be maintained, and
>
> to promote social progress and better standards of life in larger freedom,
>
> And for these ends
>
> to provide tolerance and live together in peace with one another as good neighbours, and
>
> to unite our strength to maintain international peace and security, and
>
> to ensure, by the acceptance of principles and the institution of methods, that armed forces shall not be used, save in the common interest, and
>
> to enjoy international machinery for the promotion of the economic and social advancement of all peoples.

However, unkind it might sound, the contemporary diplomats and their State authorities should reflect on the successes and/or failures of these determinations. These goals are achievable; and the States should not blame each other for derogating from their determination.

Of course, not all members of the United Nations have derogated from their determination, but a large number of them have done so. One should not maintain that these are mere pious vows. International Relations' function is to develop friendly relations between States, and to settle disputes by friendly means; but its decisions are to be legitimised by means of bilateral treaties or by diplomatic agreements, both of which are legally binding. Thus, negotiated arrangements take a legally binding form.

It is, therefore, re-iterated that the diplomats must acquire a good negotiating capacity/technique.

What was written over seventy years ago in the form of a Preamble to the UN Charter is still true; and most parts of the world, particularly, the developing world remains almost unchanged; moreover, human beings in the developing world are the victims of warfares which are particularly based on megalomania of States; thus the leaders of most of the States have failed the UN. In these circumstances the question of promoting social progress and "better standards of life in larger freedom" may never be achieved.

The Preamble to the Charter rightly advised the Member States of the United Nations to "practice tolerance and live together in peace with one another as good neighbours…," but the major parts of the world failed to observe this direction and failed the United Nations, an institution, the success of which very much depends on the conduct of the Organisation's members. If the United Nations, as a world organisation, has failed to perform its duties, the Member States must take the blame onto themselves for inaction or as unsuitable members of the organisation. This would be found by many as an unacceptable history which is chequered with warfares! But the fact remains that the United Nations has become a victim of criticisms of the international community. Many of the heads of States and their representatives, the diplomats of all categories, should review their position and be engaged in constructive plans.

Chapter I of the UN Charter details its *Purposes and Principles.* Article 1 of the Charter identified the Purposes of the United Nations which are:

Paragraph 1 of Article 1

> To maintain international peace and security, and to that end: to take effective collective measures for the prevention and removal of threats to the peace, and for the suppression of acts of aggression or other breaches of the peace, and to bring about by peaceful means, and in conformity with the principles of justice and international law, adjustment or settlement of international disputes or situations which might lead to a breach of the peace.

This Article consists of four paragraphs, each of which, except the last paragraph, requires explanation; it has therefore been decided to comment on each paragraph of the Article separately.

Paragraph 1 of the Article rightly pointed out the importance of maintaining international peace and security particularly after the effect of the two World Wars; unfortunately, wars have become such a common phenomenon almost in all parts of the developing world that the wave of which is also felt by the States in the West, particularly by the high flow of migration and very high scale of financial aid given by the rich countries and many international, inter-governmental and non-governmental institutions.

This Paragraph also recommended the Member States to "take effective collective measures for the prevention and removal of threats to the peace, and for the suppression of acts of aggression ...." But has the international community achieved it? This question should be considered seriously by the governments and their diplomats bearing in mind that the role of diplomats has changed in the contemporary world and that the attitude towards cooperation among governments is an essentially important factor for peace-making. Breach of the peace must be avoided by all means and all members of the General Assembly of the UN should refer their disputes or differences to it in the first instance.

Paragraph 2 of Article 1

> To develop friendly relations among nations based on respect for the principles of equal rights and self-determination of peoples, and to take other appropriate measures to strengthen universal peace.

Self-determination of people and to strengthen universal peace are the two major themes in this paragraph. Self-determination of people is now an established principle of international law. The people in the newly born States are not usually allowed their fundamental rights and freedoms by their State authorities; it simply defeats the purpose of self-determination. It has already been explained, albeit briefly, that given the behaviour of States, it may safely be assumed that the prospects of strengthening the foundations of universal peace have been receding.

Paragraph 3 of Article 1 stated that:

> To achieve international co-operation in solving international problems of an economic, social, cultural or humanitarian character and in promoting and encouraging respect for human rights and for fundamental freedoms for all without distinction as to race, sex, language, or religion ....

In view of the current behaviour of the majority of States, the prospects of "international co-operation in solving international problems..." would seem to be a far cry. Zartman made two interesting statements among others:

> Selfish States bury conflict if (as long as) the other party does so too, and unselfish States bury conflict because the other party does so too ... the grave is shallower for the first than for the second.[25]

Again he stated that:

> Cooperation ... occurs to create beneficial outcomes that the parties cannot create alone, but it is also needed to allocate those benefits; there is always a distributive as well as an integrative aspect to cooperation.[26]

However, briefly, in order to achieve a successful inter-State cooperation activity, the parties involved in such an activity must possess a good negotiating technique and that they must be familiar with the real causes of the so-called conflict between them and remain totally unbiased.

Paragraph 4 of the Article provided that:

> To be a center for harmonising the actions of nations in the attainment of these common ends.

The aspirations of the drafters of the UN Charter were correct; however, if the majority of the international community fails to satisfy their obligations under paragraphs 1, 2 and 3, which they unfortunately have, then the subject matter of paragraph 4 also proved to be otiose. Before concluding the Purposes of Article 1, it must be emphasised that the drafters of the UN Charter drafted it bearing in mind the miseries that the two World Wars caused to humankind; but unfortunately, the majority of the Member States are in breach of their obligations although at the time of accepting their membership of the Organisation they promised to honour their obligations.

Article 2 of the Charter contains seven paragraphs; each of these paragraphs, which represents a Principle, is now briefly examined to remind the Member States, including their heads and diplomatic representatives, of their obligations.

The Preamble to this Article states that:

[25] I W Zartman and S Touval (eds), *International Cooperation: The Extents and Limits of Multilateralism*, Cambridge, Cambridge University Press (2010) at 6.

[26] Op. cit., at 7.

> The Organization and its Members, in pursuit of the Purposes stated in Article 1, shall act in accordance with the following Principles.

Two things should be emphasised prior to examining any of the paragraphs of Article 2. First, that the members of the United Nations shall pursue the purposes of the Organisation as stated in Article 1, and secondly that these Principles are obligatory for them, by virtue of using the words, "shall act."

Principle 1

"The Organization is based on the principle of sovereign equality of all its Members."

This provision is extremely important in that from a legal standpoint, all sovereigns are equal, irrespective of their size, economic or military power. But in reality, the economic and military powers tend to dominate the smaller and less powerful States. The history of the domination of the weak by the strong is a lengthy one. It is clear now that political administrations would prefer a vertical power structure rather than a horizontal one. The irony of the matter is that the vast majority of the newly born States themselves suffer from an inferiority complex vis-à-vis the economically and militarily powerful States. There was no need for it, if only they did not allow the powerful States to dominate them, and this could be achieved if only they attained a high level of self-sufficiency by building their own capacity. But unfortunately majority of the leaders in the developing world do not seem to pay much attention to this issue.

This way the power matrix in the world could also be changed. Economic diplomacy forms the basis for foreign policy-making.[27]

Principle 2

> All Members, in order to ensure to all of them the rights and benefits resulting from membership, shall fulfil in good faith, the obligations assumed by them in accordance with the present Charter.
>
> "Shall fulfil in good faith" stands for a legally binding (in good faith) obligations assumed by them. It should be regarded as a peremptory norm—that is, a norm from which no derogation is permissible.

Principle 3

[27] See further C Chatterjee, *Economic Diplomacy and Foreign Policy-making*, New York, Palgrave Macmillan (2020).

> All Members shall settle their international disputes by peaceful means in such a manner that international peace and security and justice are not endangered.

There are two provisions on this issue; one in the UN Charter itself; and the other may be found in the Statute of the International Court of Justice. First, the UN Charter provisions should be exhausted by diplomats competently, and second the parties concerned are required to exhaust the procedures identified in Article 38 of the Statute of the International Court of Justice.

Article 33 of the UN Charter (quoted in section 8.3.3) provides that:

1. The parties to any dispute, the continuance of which is likely to endanger the maintenance of international peace and security, shall, first of all, seek a solution by negotiation, enquiry, mediation, conciliation, arbitration, judicial settlement, resort to regional agencies or arrangements, or other peaceful means of their own choice.
2. The Security Council shall, when it deems necessary, call upon the parties to settle their disputes by such means.

Paragraph 1 of Article 33 is one of the reasons for writing this chapter, as the primary purpose of this work is to emphasise that negotiating techniques learned by diplomats in the changing and challenging circumstances might be the factor for resolving a large number of international, inter-State and domestic disputes.

The drafting of Article 33 provokes certain controversies, namely "likely to endanger"—how to determine whether a dispute "the continuance of which is likely to endanger the maintenance of international peace and security"; without going into any academic controversies on this issue, the practical answer would be that it is a matter for the experts to determine whether the continuance is likely to endanger the maintenance of international peace and security. Article 47(1) of the UN Charter provides that:

> There shall be established a Military Staff Committee to advise and assist the Security Council on all questions relating to the Security Council's military requirements for the maintenance of international peace and security, the employment and command of forces placed at its disposal, the regulation of armaments, and possible disarmament.

Thus, it is a military issue and shall be confirmed on each occasion by the Military Staff Committee. Paragraph 3 of the same Article provides that:

> The Military Staff Committee shall be responsible under the Security Council for the strategic direction of any armed forces placed at the disposal of the Security Council ....

However, the second issue in Article 33(1) would be when is a "dispute" a dispute? Are there any differences between a "dispute" and a "difference"? In reality, most of the domestic inter-race disputes within a State, for example, or even the so-called inter-State disputes are, in fact, differences of opinions which are in many cases based on either misunderstanding of issues between the parties or are based on "prejudices."

Returning to the differences between "differences" and "disputes," it may be stated that a "difference" stands for a difference between two or more parties on the same issue(s)—basically factual issue(s). Incidentally, most of the differences at a domestic level are not concerned with rights of the parties, for example, differences based on race are usually unfounded.

As to "disputes," these are concerned with respective "rights" and "freedoms." Disputes are to be "justiciable," which is concerned with the rights of the parties.[28]

Thirdly, Article 33(1) has not put the methods of settling any dispute or difference, between the parties, in any order. It may however be maintained that the best procedure would be to "inquire" the causes of the differences between the parties concerned; after that "negotiation" between the parties must be the best method of settling domestic and/or inter-State differences or disputes. Then should come conciliation, and thereafter mediation, if of course, both negotiation and conciliation should unfortunately fail. In a mediation process, there hardly exists any room for interplay between the parties; they are supposed to be bound by the mediator's considered views on the subject matter of the "difference" or "dispute" between the parties concerned. If, however, each of these methods of settling differences or disputes between the parties should fail, then of

[28] For a detailed discussion of the real meaning of these terms, see H Lauterpacht, *The Function of Law in the International Community*, Archon Books, Hamden (1966), Chapter XVII at 351.

course, the issues should be referred to arbitration, judicial settlement or even to regional agency concerned to activate its dispute settlement machinery.[29]

Principle 4

> All Members shall refrain in their international relations from the threat or use of force against the territorial integrity or political independence of any State, or in any other manner inconsistent with the Purposes of the United Nations.

Ironically, many of the Member States of the UN are in breach of this Principle. This is a reminder to the heads of States concerned and their diplomats too. No criticism is intended for the diplomatic community but to remind the international community of the need for a more forward-looking diplomats to cope with the attitude of the changing world in order to ensure that no more warfares take place. The art to learn effective negotiating techniques might provide some solutions to the problem. The purpose of writing these comments is not to examine each of these Articles from an academic point of view, but simply to draw the attention of the Member States as to how they are frustrating the objectives of the UN. It is also for them to change the path of the Organisation.[30]

Principle 5

This Principle states that:

> All Members shall give the United Nations every assistance in any action it takes in accordance with the present Charter, and shall refrain from giving assistance to any State against which the United Nations is taking preventive or enforcement action.

[29] See further C Chatterjee and A Lefcovitch, *Alternative Dispute Resolution: A Practical Guide*, London, Routledge (2008); see also C Chatterjee and A Lefcovitch, "A Critical Evaluation of the UN Convention on International Settlement Agreements Resulting from Mediations 2019" 23 *Financial Regulation International*, Issue 4 (2020).

[30] For a detailed and an instructive interpretation of each of these principles, see R Higgins, op. cit., Part IV.

The above Principle is in conformity with the Preamble to the UN Charter, but this Principle has been most honoured in its breach.[31]

Principle 6 provides that:

> The Organization shall ensure that States which are not Members of the United Nations act in accordance with these Principles so far as may be necessary for the maintenance of international peace and security.

The above provision has provoked controversy in that if the Charter gives rise to contractual obligations, which it does, how may it be sustainable that non-members would be bound by its provisions? But this issue should be considered from a different standpoint.

The UN aspired to be a truly international organisation; therefore, its provision should encompass the non-member States too. Of course, at the time the UN came into operation, there were only a few States which were not members of it; furthermore, none of them was a militarily powerful State.

Principle 7

Finally, this Principle of Article 2 provides that:

> Nothing contained in the present Charter shall authorize the United Nations to intervene in matters which are essentially within the domestic jurisdiction of any State or shall require the Members to submit such matters to settlement under the present Charter; but this Principle shall not prejudice the application of enforcement measures under Chapter VII.

It has to be emphasised that the UN is not a State; it is simply a "club" so to say of the States; but these members, in order to fulfil their obligations, under the Charter have undertaken the Charter obligations. However, Principle 7 of Article 2 rightly stated that the UN has no right to "intervene" in matters "which are essentially within the domestic jurisdiction of any State." The provisions of this have of course provoked controversy particularly in regard to connotations of the term "intervene" as well as the method(s) of determining which matters may be "essentially within the domestic jurisdiction of any State." These controversies seem to be never-ending.[32]

[31] For details on this Principle, please consult R Higgins, op. cit.

[32] For a thorough discussion of these issues, see R Higgins, op. cit., *The Development of International Law through the Political Organs of the United Nations*, op. cit

It is unreservedly maintained that despite the above discussion of the Preamble to the UN Charter, its Purposes and Principles have not been discussed in depth; but that was not the principal purpose of writing this chapter. Its main purpose is to familiarise students of diplomatic studies or even the junior members of the diplomatic community with the basic objectives and purposes of the United Nations. Days are changing too fast; it is for them to modify the current practice of the UN and its main organs, if and where necessary, rather than undermining the Organisation and its Specialised Agencies. Secondly, it should also be emphasised once again that the dispute settlement methods as provided for by Article 33, paragraph 1, should be seriously considered by the diplomatic community and learn them. Of all the methods recommended by this Article it is felt that the negotiating techniques should be essentially learned by the diplomatic community especially in view of the ever-changing world.

Finally, it is also to be emphasised that war begets war; let us give peace a chance to change this war-torn world.

At this stage, it would be appropriate to briefly discuss the principal organs of the United Nations and some of its Specialised Agencies. It is again iterated that the purpose is not to become comprehensive on this task but to introduce to the young diplomatic community the primary functions of these organs and Agencies.[33]

Chapter III of the UN Charter (Article 7) mentions the principal organs of the United Nations. These are:

a General Assembly;
a Security Council;
an Economic and Social Council;
a Trusteeship Council;
an International Court of Justice; and
a Secretariat

Paragraph 2 of Article 7 states that:

> Such subsidiary organs as may be found necessary may be established in accordance with the present Charter.

[33] For a detailed discussion of UN organs and its Specialised Agencies, see R Higgins, op. cit.,; M N Shaw, *International Law*, Cambridge, Cambridge |University Press (latest edition) and Bowett's *Law of International Institutions*, Sands and Klein (eds), London, Sweet & Maxwell (latest edition).

Article 8, although not entirely relevant in this context, it is nevertheless important to quote:

> The United Nations shall place no restrictions on the eligibility of men and women to participate in any capacity and under conditions of equality in its principal and subsidiary organs.

This message is important particularly for the developing States. Equal participation of men and women in public offices would be a direct means of "capacity-building."

Chapter IV of the UN Charter which has been developed over 14 Articles (Articles 9–22) related to the *General Assembly*. Again, the purpose is not to detail the powers and functions of the General Assembly, but only to briefly highlight some of its important aspects and functions. The name of this organ is significant—it is a general, not a special organ, and that it is the platform at which all the members of the UN meet to discuss issues and matters of international concern. No member may bring more than five representatives to this platform on any occasion.

This brings one back to some of the basic qualities that diplomats attending such a platform should possess after appropriate training and participate there constructively. A diplomat, as stated earlier, must be articulate in expressing himself/herself in one of the official languages of the United Nations. He/she must also be extremely familiar with the issues and matters that may be under discussion. At such a stage a diplomat should not suffer from any complex whether he/she represents a developing country or a developed country. If the issue/matter is of an international concern such as the climate change or protection and preservation of the environment, then diplomats should reach a consensus which would be agreed to by the majority of the members present and voting.

Under Article 10, the General Assembly "may discuss any question or any matter within the scope of the present Charter or relating to the powers and functions of any organs provided for in the present Charter … may make recommendations to the Members of the United Nations or to the Security Council or to both on any such question or matter." Thus, the General Assembly has been given a very broad jurisdiction to discuss any question or any matter provided it is within the scope of the UN Charter. It has also the authority to make recommendations to the members of the UN or to the Security Council or to both on any such question or matter.

The General Assembly can also consider the general principles of cooperation in the maintenance of international peace and security "... including the principles governing disarmament and the regulation of armaments ...." There is little point in disregarding the activities of the General Assembly, including the binding nature of its resolutions, in whichever form they may be published, bearing in mind that it may not be compared with a national legislative body. The UN is an association of States, which offers them to discuss a variety of issues and matters; and there is no reason why its resolutions may not be treated as legally binding.[34]

The diplomatic community is now required to appreciate that unless enforcement action by the Security Council has proved to be essential, there is no reason why every important issue or matter may not be referred to the UN General Assembly to reach a consensus, and all members of it should accept this result as a binding obligation for them.

It is also important to remember that under Article 12 of the Charter "The Secretary-General with the consent of the Security Council, shall notify the General Assembly at each session of any matter relative to the maintenance of international peace and security which are being dealt with by the Security Council and shall notify the General Assembly ...." The diplomatic community may like to depart from the traditional view that the General Assembly holds a secondary position; that the Security Council is the supreme authority under the UN system; it is supreme in the sense that it holds enforcement power. It is clear that the General Assembly offers the members of the UN the platform to discuss and consider the gravity of all issues and matters in the world, and yet the work of this organ is often undermined.

Article 13 of the Charter allows the General Assembly to initiate studies and make recommendations for the purpose of promoting "international cooperation in the political field and encouraging the progressive development of international law and its codification." This authority of the General Assembly should be enough to establish its position within the UN system. It can also initiate studies and make recommendations in order to promote international cooperation in the economic, social, cultural, educational and health fields. The General Assembly may also recommend measures for the peaceful adjustment of any situation, which in

[34] See further F B Sloan, op. cit.

its opinion is "likely to impair the general welfare or friendly relations among nations ..." (Article 14).

It is for the General Assembly to receive and consider annual and special reports from the Security Council; from this standpoint, the Security Council is accountable to the General Assembly (Article 15). The General Assembly also receives and considers reports from the other organs of the United Nations.

Under Article 17 of the UN Charter, the General Assembly considers and approves the budget of the entire Organisation. Furthermore, the expenses of the Organisation shall be borne by the members "as apportioned by the General Assembly." Article 17, paragraph 1, provides that:

> The expenses of the Organization shall be borne by the Members or apportioned by the General Assembly.[35]

In the *Certain Expenses* case a dispute arose in connection with the financing of the UN operations in the Congo and also on the deployment of the UN Emergency Force in the Middle East. Some of the Members of the UN, including two permanent members of the Security Council, namely France and then the Soviet Union, maintained that the expenses sought for by the General Assembly did not constitute expenses of the Organisation within the meaning of Article 17(2) of the Charter and refused payment.

This matter was referred to the International Court of Justice, and by a majority of nine votes to five, the Court found that such expenditures were in fact expenses within Article 17(2) of the Charter of the UN.

The Court justified its decision by pointing out that the operations were undertaken to fulfil one of the basic purposes of the United Nations; that is, to reach a solution to a dispute between the parties as soon as possible. In this case, the Secretary-General appropriately exercised his authority in incurring financial obligations of the UN, and that the expenses resulting from such operations must be considered expenses of the Organisation within the meaning of Article 17, paragraph 2, of the Charter of the UN.

The General Assembly has also the authority to consider and approve any financial and budgetary arrangements with the Specialised Agencies (administrative budgets) of the UN.

[35] See *Certain Expenses of the United Nations* Case, *ICJ Reports* (1962) at 151.

The General Assembly's authority over budgetary matters is quite extensive. Article 19 of the UN Charter provides that:

> A Member of the United Nations which is in arrears in the payment of its financial contributions to the Organization shall have no vote in the General Assembly if the amount of its arrears equals or exceeds the amount of the contributions due from it for the preceding two full years. The General Assembly may, nevertheless, permit such a Member to vote if it is satisfied that the failure to pay is due to conditions beyond the control of the Member.

A formidable power has been allowed to the General Assembly by Article 19. Without naming the Member States, it may be mentioned that quite a number of them have fallen into arrears, yet they are allowed to vote in the General Assembly. Instead of undermining the General Assembly, both the member community and the diplomatic community should pay attention to provisions such as those embodied in Article 19.

Chapter V of the UN Charter details the Powers and Functions of the Security Council. This Chapter consists of 29 Articles (Articles 23–51). It has been developed over three Chapters:

Chapter V	The Security Council
Chapter VI	Pacific Settlement of Disputes
Chapter VII	Action with Respect to Threats to the Peace, Breaches to the Peace, and Acts of Aggression

The Security Council

Article 23: Composition of the Council

The Security Council consists of eleven members. The permanent members are the Republic of China, France, the Union of Soviet Socialist Republics (now Russia), the United Kingdom of Great Britain and Northern Ireland and the United States of America. The General Assembly elects six other members of the United Nations to be non-permanent members of the Council. Incidentally, in view of their records of torture of human beings, Germany and Japan were not accepted as permanent members of the Security Council. The non-permanent members are elected for a term of two years. A retiring member may not stand for immediate re-election. "Each Member of the Security Council shall have one representative."[36]

Articles 24–26 deal with the functions and powers of the Security Council. In order to ensure prompt and effective action (not measures) by the United Nations, its members conferred on the Security Council primary responsibility for the maintenance of international peace and security, and that the members of the United Nations agreed that the Council shall act on their behalf, on condition however that in discharging these duties the Council acts in accordance with the Purposes and Principles of the United Nations. The extent of these powers may be found in Chapters VI, VII and VIII of the Charter. However, the Security Council is required to submit annual and, when necessary, special reports to the General Assembly for its consideration.

Under Article 25, the members of the United Nations agreed to accept and carry out the decisions of the Security Council. The Security Council shall remain responsible for the regulation of armaments with the assistance of the Military Staff Committee. In fact, one of the objectives of Article 26 is to promote the establishment of international peace and security "... with the least diversion for armaments of the world's human and economic resources."[37] But whatever excuses may be put forward, the harsh fact remains that the international community has been required to live in war conditions.

Article 27 provides the voting procedures to which the Security Council is subject. Each member of the Security Council has one vote. Decisions of the Security Council on procedural matters are made by an affirmative vote of seven members. The Security Council's decisions on all other matters are made by an affirmative vote of seven members of which it would include the concurring votes of the permanent members too; however, in taking decisions under Chapter VI of the Charter (Pacific Settlement of Disputes) and under paragraph 3 of Article 52 (re: Pacific Settlement of Disputes by Regional Arrangements) a party to a dispute must abstain from voting.

<u>Matters of Procedure</u>

The Council functions continuously; thus, its members are required to be represented "at all times" at the seat of the Organisation (which is New York). The Council holds periodic meetings "... at which each of its

[36] Article 23, paragraph 3.
[37] Article 26.

members may, if it so desires, be represented by a member of the government or by some other specially designated representative."[38]

The Council is allowed to hold meetings at places other than the seat of the Council (New York) if, in its opinion, another location would best facilitate its work. It has also the authority to establish any subsidiary organs as it may deem "necessary for the performance of its functions."[39] The Council has adopted its own rules of procedures and the method of selecting its president.

If a member of the United Nations which is not a member of the Security Council wishes to participate at one of its meetings, may do so, without vote, in the discussion of a question brought before the Council, provided that the Council considers that otherwise "the interests of that Member would be particularly affected."[40]

In the event of a UN member not being a member of the Security Council or even a State not being a member of the United Nations (the latter in a limited number of cases), but is a party to a dispute which is under consideration by the Security Council, shall be invited to the discussion relevant to the dispute, without vote, of course. The Security Council has the authority to lay down such conditions as it deems just for the participation of such a State.[41]

Chapter VI—*Pacific Settlement of Disputes*

This Chapter has been developed over six Articles (Articles 33–38). A basic analysis of Article 33 has already been provided. However, in the context of this Chapter, it is opportune to re-iterate that the young diplomatic community, in particular, should indeed learn the art of negotiation and conciliation even prior to their considering resorting to judicial means—one of the basic themes of this work. As the contents of Article 33 have already been analysed, there is thus no need for analysing them again.

Article 34

Under this Article, the Security Council may investigate any dispute or any situation which, according to it, might lead to an international friction or may give rise to a dispute, or to determine whether the continuance of a dispute or situation is likely to endanger the maintenance of international peace and security.

[38] Article 28, paragraph 2.

[39] Article 29.

[40] Article 31.

[41] Article 32.

This is where diplomats should discuss such issues not only with their respective governments but also within the world diplomatic community and of course cooperate with the efforts to be made by the Security Council in order to avoid any breaches of the peace or acts of aggression. Incidentally, a "situation" may present much more difficulty to determine its ultimate outcome than an actual dispute. Wars must be avoided by all means.

Article 35

Any member or even non-member of the United Nations may bring any dispute or situation (as referred to in Article 34) to the attention of the Security Council or the General Assembly for a peaceful settlement of it. Of course, in the event of a non-member of the United Nations bringing any dispute to the Security Council or the General Assembly, to which it is a party, it will be required to accept "the obligations of pacific settlement provided for in the present Charter" (Article 35). But in such a situation, if a dispute is brought to the attention of the General Assembly by a non-member State of the UN, the proceedings of the Assembly will be subject to the provisions of Articles 11 and 12 (which Articles have already been analysed in this chapter).

Article 36

Under this Article, the Security Council may, at any stage of a dispute or in resolving a situation, recommend appropriate procedures or methods of adjustment. However, it "should take into consideration any procedures for the settlement of the dispute which have already been exhausted by the parties" (Article 36, paragraph (2)). In making its recommendations under this Article, the Security Council "should also take into consideration that legal disputes should, as a general rule, be referred by the parties to the International Court of Justice."

Article 37

If however the parties to a dispute of nature referred to in Article 33 fail to settle it by the means referred to in the latter Article, they are then required to refer it to the Security Council. Should the Security Council deem that the continuance of a dispute might endanger the maintenance of peace and security then it shall decide "whether to take action under Article 36 or to recommend such terms of settlement as it may consider appropriate."[42]

[42] Article 37, paragraph (2).

The Security Council also has the authority to make recommendations to the parties for a pacific settlement of the dispute, provided the parties concerned to a dispute have requested the Security Council to that effect.

One can easily see that the balance tilts towards pacific settlement of disputes; thus the representatives of the parties concerned, the chosen officers of the States concerned and their diplomats must possess good command over the methods of settlement recommended by Article 33 of the UN Charter. But unfortunately, many of the members of the United Nations seem to have forgotten or deliberately decided to resort to warfares in the name of settling disputes between themselves, and thus, are in breach of their Charter obligations.

Chapter VII—*Action with Respect to Threats to the Peace, Breaches to the Peace, and Acts of Aggression*

This Chapter has been developed over 13 Articles (Articles 39–51). This Chapter provisions will only be effected if the Pacific Settlement of Disputes (Chapter VI provisions) fails. This is an alarming situation in that the members and even non-members who are parties to a dispute or difference did not try their best to settle their dispute/difference amicably; in other words, they believed in the Chapter VII action, which should be avoided by all means.

According to Article 39, the Security Council has the authority to determine "the existence of any threat to the peace, breach of the peace or act of aggression, and thereafter shall make recommendations, or may decide what measures (not action) shall be taken under Articles 41 and 42 of the Charter in order to maintain or restore international peace and security."

In order not to aggravate the situation (which is more worrying than an actual event) the Security Council shall try its best to avoid taking any action; thus, even before any recommendations being made or deciding on what measures (not action), in accordance with Article 39, may be taken, it is usually the most desirable provisional measures to give the parties another opportunity not to be involved in warfares. The Security Council will also have another opportunity to know why the parties failed to comply with the recommended provisional measures.

Under *Article 41* the Security Council may decide on the nature of measures (not action) not involving deployment of armed forces in order to give effect to its decisions, and also may call upon the Members of the UN to apply the recommended measures. In other words, application of forces must be avoided by all means, and its deployment would be the last resort. However, these measures usually include "complete or partial interruption of economic relations and of rail, sea, air, postal, telegraphic, radio and other means of communication (the internet may be in the present time) and the severance of diplomatic relations." This type of sanction will be disastrous for economy, including inter-State trade. This is another reason why this work has placed importance in giving training at least to the young generation of diplomats in order to ensure, with the consent of the heads of States, to request the other parties to a dispute not to force the Security Council either to impose sanctions or go into warfares. But that has not been happening effectively.

In the event of the Security Council considering that the measures recommended in Article 41 would be inadequate, or have already proved to be so, it may then take "such action by air, sea, or land forces as may be necessary to maintain or restore international peace and security. Such action may include demonstrations, blockade, and other operations by air, sea or land forces of Members of the United Nations."[43]

Of course, once the Security Council has taken action under Article 42, all members of the United Nations in order to ensure the maintenance of international peace and security undertake to make available to the Security Council armed forces assistance, including right of passage of different types of transport with their special agreement or agreements.[44] By the same token, Security Council, when it has decided to use force, may also invite a Member State which is not represented on it "to participate in the decisions of the Security Council concerning the employment of contingents of that Member's armed forces."[45]

In the context of this work, there is little point in going into the details of military action to be taken by the Security Council under Chapter VII of the Charter along with the members of the UN, or even non-members when they have so agreed. It is firmly believed that domestic differences between people of different origins or inter-State differences/disputes may be effectively resolved by negotiation and/or conciliation, which methods have also been referred to in Article 33 of the UN Charter.

[43] Article 42.
[44] Article 43.
[45] Article 44.

However, Article 51 needs to be discussed briefly to examine when a matter, at least during its initial stage, may fall within the exclusive jurisdiction of the State concerned. The Security Council must be informed as soon as possible in order to enable it to take appropriate measures to maintain international peace and security.

Article 51 provides that:

> Nothing in the present Charter shall impair the inherent right of individual or collective self-defence if an armed attack occurs against a Member of the United Nations, until the Security Council has taken measures necessary to maintain international peace and security. Measures taken by Members in the exercise of the right of self-defence shall be immediately reported to the Security Council and shall not in any way affect the authority and responsibility of the Security Council under the present Charter to take at any time such action as it deems necessary in order to maintain or restore international peace and security.

Two points should be stated rather briefly in this context: (a) that the inherent right of individual self-defence is recognised by the criminal law of States, in general; it is a municipal law concept; but has formed part of customary international law; and (b) as Higgins pointed out that "defence of the self cannot be collective, though there may exist collective security or mutual aid."[46]

At present none of the regional arrangements, which is the subject matter of Articles 52 and 53, seems to be active in regard to matters relating to the maintenance of international peace and security. Nevertheless the Association of South East Asian Nations (ASEAN) seems to be quite successful in regard to regional trade and investment issues.

Chapter X of the Charter deals with an important organ of the United Nations—the Economic and Social Council (ECOSOC). In the context of this work, it is important to draw the attention of the reader to the powers and functions of this organ of the UN, as diplomats and the Member States of the UN have an enormous duty to perform for the success of the UN as well as this Organ.

[46] See R Higgins, op. cit., at 208–209; Bowett maintained that collective self-defence may exist only where the interest of an aggressed State is so closely bound up with the territorial integrity and political independence of a neighbouring State. In other words "geographical proximity and politico-economic interests of the two States are intrinsically bound." See D W Bowett, 32 *British Year Book of International Law* (1955–56) at 130.

Although this Chapter contains 12 Articles (Articles 61–72), in the context of this work, Article 62 entitled Functions and Powers is the most important one with which all heads of States, members of the United Nations and their diplomats should be familiar. Incidentally, each member of the Economic and Social Council shall have one representative.

Article 62 (Functions and Powers) provides that:

1. The Economic and Social Council may make or initiate studies and reports with respect to international economic, social, cultural, educational, health and related matters and make recommendations with respect to any such matter to the General Assembly, to the Members of the United Nations, and to the specialised agencies concerned.
2. It may make recommendations for the purpose of promoting respect for and observance of human rights and fundamental freedoms for all.
3. It may prepare draft Conventions for submission to the General Assembly, with respect to matters falling within its competence.
4. It may call, in accordance with the rules prescribed by the United Nations, international conferences on matters falling within its competence.

Article 62 of the UN Charter is an extensive Article to detail the objectives and functions of the Economic and Social Council, and there is no need to go into any other Articles which are mostly procedural in nature (Articles 63–72), Article 61, in the context of this work, need not be examined critically.

The Member States of the UN and their diplomats should take advantage of the provisions of Article 62 by prompting the ECOSOC to initiate studies which would add to the socio-economic development process; they can also prepare draft Conventions for submission to the General Assembly. In a very changing world, the scope of Article 62 may cover many issues only if the Member States of the UN and their diplomats take the initiative to utilise the ECOSOC in its full potentials.

Chapter XV of the UN Charter deals with the Secretariat. It consists of five Articles (Articles 97–101). A brief analysis of the Secretariat is thought to be useful for members of the UN and their diplomats. It comprises a Secretary-General and such staff as the Organisation (the UN) may require. The Secretary-General is appointed by the General Assembly upon the recommendation of the Security Council. He is the Chief Administrative Officer of the Organisation.

The Secretary-General acts in that capacity in all meetings of the General Assembly, of the Security Council, of the ECOSOC, and performs such other functions as may be entrusted to him by these organs. He also makes an annual report to the General Assembly of the work of the Organisation.[47]

He may also draw the attention of the Security Council on any matter "which in his opinion threatens the maintenance of international peace and security."[48]

In order to maintain a neutral position, Article 100 of the UN Charter provides that in the performance of their duties, the Secretary-General and the staff "shall not seek or receive instructions from any government or from any other authority external to the Organization. They shall refrain from any action which might reflect on their position as international officials responsible only to the Organization."[49]

In the context of this work, it has been decided to quote, in full, the contents of paragraph (2) of Article 100:

> Each Member of the United Nations undertakes to respect the exclusively international character of the responsibilities of the Secretary-General and the staff and not to seek to influence them in the discharge of their responsibilities.

The Secretary-General holds a very important position, and may also initiate or provide suggestions for improvements in the maintenance of international peace and security and socio-economic development.[50]

The Trusteeship Council which was established after the end of the Second World War with a view to supervising the trust territories (mandated territories, and areas separated from the enemy States, and certain other territories which were voluntarily placed under the trusteeship system) was abolished a few years ago. Incidentally, the only former mandated territory, which was not placed under the trusteeship system, was South West Africa. After the independence of Palau, the last trust territory,

[47] Article 98.

[48] Article 99.

[49] Article 100, paragraph (1).

[50] See, for example, *An Agenda for Peace* by Dr Boutros-Ghali which was adopted by the Summit Meeting of the Security Council on 31 January 1992, New York; see also *In Larger Freedom* by Kofi Annan, A/59/2005.

on 1 October 1994, the Council suspended its operation (not abolished as it required an amendment to the UN Charter) on 1 November 1994.[51]

It would be out of the context of this work to discuss the International Court of Justice.

8.5 Conclusions

As stated earlier that by accepting the membership of the United Nations, each of the members undertook the obligations to implement its policies, whether they were expressed as decisions, resolutions, conventions, recommendations, charters, declarations or whatever. It has been emphasised in this chapter that the UN is not a law-making body in the municipal law sense; it can render directions under various titles.

Thus, the UN's guidelines in whichever form they might be published, its members may find it useful to observe rather than setting bad examples, which eventually may lead to warfares, which must be avoided by all means, and utilise the UN in accordance with their membership obligations.

In this chapter all the organs of the UN have been discussed briefly; not all statements made in respect of these organs have been supported by case law, as this might have the effect of distancing diplomats from this work.

Two issues may be especially identified in this connection: (a) that the permanent members of the Security Council were chosen and elected in 1945. Days have significantly changed since then; the question now is whether the Member States and their diplomatic community should revise the permanent membership structure of the Council by rotating permanent members of it. At present, the Security Council membership structure is too politically and militarily charged and that defeats the philosophy on which the UN was founded; (b) the veto power should be accorded to the non-permanent members of it too[52]; this might encourage them to take more interest in the UN activities; indeed it will be in conformity with the equal treatment principle of the Charter.

It should be emphasised in this context that people, in general, tend to evaluate the UN by referring to the activities of the Security Council,

[51] For information on the composition and functions of the Trusteeship Council, see Chapters XI and XII of the UN Charter.

[52] Currently, of the ten non-permanent members of the Security Council, five are allocated to the Afro-Asian States, one to Eastern Europe, two to Latin America and two to Western European and other States; see the UNGA Resolution 1991 (XVIII).

without appreciating that the activities of the General Assembly and the Economic and Social Council are very important too. The diplomatic community should closely study their work, and actively participate in them which would enhance the socio-economic development process particularly in the developing parts of the world.

The United Nations have been with us since 1945 (24 October); it is over seventy-five years now that the international community, in general, has mostly abused this universal institution and criticised it in its own way. Time has now come for the community to think how this organisation could be utilised even better so that international peace and security could be maintained in a more friendly way and improved through appropriate cooperation with this organisation, and at the same time improve the governance systems particularly in the developing world.

CHAPTER 9

Conclusions

In this work an attempt has been made to demonstrate how prudent negotiating techniques may be extremely fruitful in both diplomacy and in regard to commercial matters. It is important that both diplomats and people engaged in negotiating commercial contracts of various types should have special expertise in this discipline rather than maintaining they have expertise in these disciplines.

It is important to bear in mind that both the diplomatic and the commercial world including private foreign investment scenario are changing fast, and also that the experts in the developing countries are now learning what they want for themselves, and they are often opposed to submitting themselves to the dominant parties. Some of these countries do have now quite strong economies and the so-called notion of bargaining power is no longer valid.

It is also believed that women, properly trained, may also be good negotiators, and the best example to confirm this statement would be how women are being included in negotiating parties to settle both commercial and non-commercial matters. Indeed, a chapter on how women in developing countries, particularly in the rural areas of these countries, may be empowered to participate in negotiating techniques, in addition to providing ideas on how women's human reserves may add to the reservoir of human resources in the country has been added to this work.

C. Chatterjee, *Negotiating Techniques in Diplomacy and Business Contracts*, https://doi.org/10.1007/978-3-030-81732-9_9

This work has also suggested how through the process of responsible negotiations, dependency of developing countries on the traditionally rich countries may be minimised.

Both the diplomatic world and the diplomats should appreciate that the world of diplomacy is changing fast due to the new trading patterns and the nature of private foreign investments, the uses of technology and the new idea of making a global economy.

What is urgently needed is to enhance the capacity-building of the developing countries according to their priorities, which should allow them to have deeper knowledge in manufacturing goods and providing services. The issues of countertrade, barter, counter-purchase and so on rather than producing cash-based payments[1] should also receive the diplomat's attention.

The UN system rightly promoted the concept of friendly settlement of disputes, and in particular, the method(s) of operating this kind of diplomacy has been described in Article 33 of the UN Charter, which has received attention in this work. But unfortunately, history has repeated itself; the UN objectives particularly in regard to peace-making have failed owing to the failure of some of the UN members, who seem to have disregarded the techniques of settling societal conflicts and the conflicts between States. This is where diplomats need sophisticated training in negotiating techniques and conciliations. There is no point in re-iterating the adverse effect of warfares; human sufferings become immeasurable. This happens most often owing to power-mongering or because of racial hatred between societies. The UN Charter has provided for all kinds of remedies, and yet, many of the members, despite their obligations towards the UN simply disregarded the Organisation. The UN Charter has the characteristics of a contract. Each of its members signed this Charter in good faith; but many of them are in breach of their obligation. A simple attempt to seek the UN's suggestions will not do; they are required to engage the UN in settling disputes. It is repeated that wars are no alternatives to peace; and it is one of the duties of diplomats to convince their governments accordingly in order to attain peace.

Diplomacy is a very old institution, and the method of choosing diplomats befitted the old world. They were, in general, chosen from aristocratic families who were familiar with etiquettes and manners, and they, in general, had the gift of the gab too. Their principal function was to

[1] See further C Chatterjee, *Legal Aspects of Trade Finance*, London Routledge (2006).

establish rapport primarily on a bilateral basis with the neighbouring countries and also those of the countries which would be useful for trade and commerce, which is currently known as economic diplomacy. In the olden days diplomats were not governed by any written Code of Conduct or any international convention.

Interestingly enough, with the advent of a large number of States, as a direct result of de-colonisation process after the end of the Second World War, the Vienna Convention on Diplomatic Relations was concluded in 1961, which was followed by the Vienna Convention on Consular Relations, 1963; both these Conventions formalised the techniques of developing inter-State relations, including the rules of developing consular relations between States in a formal way.

But then, in the olden days, diplomats were also engaged in war diplomacy, but unfortunately, it did not prove to be sufficiently effective; after the First World War the League of Nations was established, but it failed to abolish warfares altogether.

It is important to appreciate that not only the old-fashioned ideas of diplomacy are over, but also the dynamics of it have been changing particularly over the past two decades. Diplomats are therefore required to keep pace with the new dynamics of diplomacy as it may change. Most of all, in order to avoid warfares, they should be required to learn negotiating techniques in respect of all aspects of diplomacy, and establish a revised foundation of peace.

The international community (both developed and developing countries) is required to consider whether the General Assembly should insist on the parties arriving at a negotiated conclusion prior to their submitting their disputes to a mediator or to the International Court of Justice. Diplomatic solutions to the differences between the parties as indicated by Article 33 of the Charter should be reached by negotiation and conciliation. However, prior to their referring their differences/disputes to make further attempts for a meaningful negotiation and conciliation process, the parties should fully participate under the supervision of a qualified negotiator or conciliator. The mediation process entails what may be described as an imposition of the mediator's decision on the disputant parties, which process often fails.[2]

[2] See further C Chatterjee and A Lefcovitch, *Alternative Dispute Resolution: A Practical Guide*, London Routledge (2008).

It is further maintained that the international community, in general, including its diplomatic community, may like to reflect on their attitudes towards the lack of the legally binding effect of the various guidelines that the UN organs, and in particular, the General Assembly, render from time to time. The use of the Security Council should be as infrequent as possible. The diplomatic community must make all efforts to utilise the services and guidelines that the UN General Assembly might offer to reach a peaceful settlement of disputes, although under Chapter VI of the Charter, the Security Council is to take measures progressively, but the aggressive Member States, in many cases, with external military support, often violate the established principles of international law. This should be stopped.

Traditional diplomacy was primarily confined to developing friendly relations with other States, depending upon their commercial status. But modern-day diplomacy is not only concerned with trade diplomacy but also with socio-economic issues, and even warfares which disturb, if not destroy, the societies causing very extensive miseries to humankind. On behalf of their governments, diplomats are now required to be involved in peace-making and socio-economic development process along with the United Nations and their regional bodies, where they are still active.

A few decades ago what was solely considered to be a domestic issue guarded by the States concerned, by their public policy and sovereignty, is no longer to be treated so. Denial of fundamental rights to the nationals and residents living within their jurisdictions, non-observance of the duty to protect or denial of justice by judicial bodies are no longer to be treated as exclusively matters of domestic jurisdictions.

Although appointed by their governments, diplomats should be allowed to advise on truly non-domestic issues after notifying their governments, and where necessary, on domestic issues too. They must therefore possess extensive knowledge on a variety of issues which may adversely affect the international community and develop policies for this community so that the resources which are spent on non-profitable issues may be diverted to the causes of the international community. It is not nice to see that many corporate entities and States are still promoting slavery and slave trade either directly or through their corporate entities or promoting cyber-crimes by failing to take preventative measures or even money laundering across national boundaries to name but a few.

As stated above that with the changing dynamics of diplomacy, diplomats and their governments are now required to look at the issues of the international community to match this changing dynamics.

Bibliography and Additional Reading

Aust, A. "The Law of State Immunity", 51 *International and Comparative Law Quarterly* (2004) at 255.

Bentwich, N. and Martin, A. *A Commentary on the Charter of the United Nations*, London, Macmillan (1951).

Berridge, G. R. *Diplomacy: Theory and Practice*, New York, Palgrave Macmillan (2010).

Boutros-Ghali, B. "An Agenda for Peace", UN (1992).

Brett, R. and Specht, I. *Young Soldiers: Why They Choose To Fight*, Boulder, Lynne Rienner Publishers (2004).

Burton, J. W. "Peace Begins at Home—International Conflict: A Domestic Responsibility", 6 *International Journal of Peace Studies*, vol. 6, no.7 at 5.

Chatterjee, C. *Negotiating Techniques in International Commercial Contracts*, Aldershot, Ashgate (2000).

———. "The Reality of Risks in Private Foreign Investment" *International Company and Commercial Law Review* (January 1996).

———. *Legal Aspects of Trade Finance*, London, Routledge (2006).

———. "Recognition and Enforcement of Arbitral Awards: How Effective is Article V of the New York Convention of 1958?" *International In-house Counsel Journal* Vol. 9, No. 36, Summer (2016), 1.

———. "Procedural Aspects of Project Finance" 8 *Journal of International Banking Law* (1993) at 421.

———. *Economic Diplomacy and Foreign Policy-making*, New York, Palgrave Macmillan (2020).

Chatterjee, C. and Lefcovitch, A. *Alternative Dispute Resolution; A Practical Guide*, London, Routledge (2008).

C. Chatterjee, *Negotiating Techniques in Diplomacy and Business Contracts*, https://doi.org/10.1007/978-3-030-81732-9

Cockett, R. *Sudan: Darfur and the Failure of an African State*, New Haven, Yale University Press (2010).

Cohen, H. "The Responsibility of the Successor State for War Debts", 44 *American Journal of International Law* (1950) at 477.

Cohen, R. "Negotiating Across Cultures", Washington, DC, US Institute of Peace Press (2007).

Collier, P. *The Bottom Billion: Why the Poorest Countries Are Failing and What Can Be Done About It?* Oxford, Oxford University Press (2008) at 34–35.

Easterly, W. "Democratic Accountability in Development: The Double Standard", 77 *Social Research*, No.4 at 1076.

Eichstaedt, P. "Kony 20Never—Inside the mind of Africa's Most Wanted Man", *Foreign Affairs* (2014).

Eltringham, N et al. (eds.). "Debating the Rwandan Genocide" in P Kaarsholm (ed.), *Violence, Political Culture and Development in Africa*, Oxford, Oxford University Press (2006).

Evatt, H. V. *The UN*, Oxford, Oxford University Press (1948).

Fitzmaurice, G. "State Immunity from Proceedings in Foreign Courts", 14 *British Year Book of International Law* (1933) 101.

Fourth World Conference. The Beijing Declaration and Platform for Action (1995).

Fox, H. and Webb, P. *The Law of State Immunity*, Oxford, Oxford University Press (latest edition).

Gezon, L. L. "Marriage, Kin and Compensation: A Socio-Political Ecology of Gender in Ankarana, Madagascar", *Anthropological Quarterly*, vol.75 no.4, (2002), pp 675–706.

Goodrich, L. and Hambro, E. *Charter of the United Nations: Commentary and Documents*, New York, Columbia University Press (1969).

Goodspeed, S. S. *International Organization, The Nature and Function of International Organisation*, New York, Oxford University Press (1959).

Green, L. C. *International Law Through the Cases*, London, Stevens & Sons Ltd (1970).

Hartman, F. H. *The Relations of Nations*, New York, Macmillan (1962).

Harvard Business Press Services. "Winning Negotiations: That Preserve Relationships" (2004).

Higgins, R. "The Concept of Domestic Jurisdiction in United Nations Practice, *The Development of International Law Through the Political Organs of the United Nations*", Oxford, Oxford University Press (1963).

———. "Certain Unresolved Aspects of the Law of State Immunity", 29 *Netherlands International Law Review* (1982) at 265.

———. *Problems and Process International Law and How We Use It*, Oxford, Oxford University Press (1995).

———. *The Development of International Law Through the Political Organs of the United Nations*, Oxford, Oxford University Press (1963b).

Huntington, S. P. *The Clash of Civilizations and the Remaking of World Order*, New York, Simon and Schuster (2011).

Jennings, R. Y, and Watts, A. D. Oppenheim's International Law, vol. I, Oxford, Oxford University Press (1992) at 341.

Kant, I. *Kant's Principles of Politics: Including His Essay on Perpetual Peace* (1891), Translated by W Hastie, Massachusetts, Kessinger Publishing (2010); see also J Burton, op. cit.

Keen, D. "Incentives and Disincentives for Violence" in M Berdal and D Malone (eds.), *Greed and Grievance: Economic Agendas in Civil Wars*, Boulder, Lynne Rienner Publishers (2000).

Kelsen, H. *Law of the United Nations*, London, Stevens (1950).

Lauterpacht, H. *The Function of Law in the International Community*, Archon Books, Hamden (1966).

Maddux, R. B. *Successful Negotiation*, London, Kogan Page (1988).

Mann, M. *The Dark Side of Democracy: Explaining Ethnic Cleansing*, Cambridge, Cambridge University Press (2005).

Mohanty, C. T. "Under Western Eyes, Feminism and Colonial Discourse", *Feminist Review*, vol. 30, no.3, (1988), pp. 61–88.

Momsen, J. H. *Gender and Development*, London, Routledge (2004) at 14.

Murray, C. and Holloway, D., et al. (eds.). Schmitthoff's The Law and Practice of International Trade, London, Sweet & Maxwell, latest edition (2007).

Nicholas, H. G. *The United Nations as a Political Institution*, Oxford, Oxford University Press (1962).

Nussbaum, M. C. *Women and Human Development: The Capabilities Approach*, New York, Cambridge University Press (2000) at 106.

Nye, J. *Understanding International Conflicts: An Introduction to Theory and History*, New York, Pearson Longman (2005).

O'Connell, D. P. *International Law*, vol. 1, London, Stevens (1970).

Paris, R. *At War's End: Building Peace After Civil Conflict*, Cambridge, Cambridge University Press (2004).

Sands, P. and Klein, P. (eds.). *Bowett's Law of International Institutions*, London, Sweet & Maxwell (latest edition) (2009).

Schreuer, C. H. *State Immunity: Some Recent Developments*, Cambridge, Cambridge University Press (1988).

Sen, A. *Development As Freedom*, New York, Random House (1993).

Shaw, M. *International Law*, Cambridge, Cambridge University Press, latest edition (2012).

Sinclair, I. The Law of Sovereign Immunity: Recent Developments, 167 Hague Recueil (1980) at 113.

Sloan, B. "The Binding Force of a Recommendation of the General Assembly of the UN", 25 *British Year Book of International Law* (1948) 1.

Sucharitkul, S. *State Immunities and Trading Activities in International Law*, New York, Praeger (1960).
The Office of the UN Special on Gender Issues and Advancement of Women, UN Supporting Gender Mainstreaming, New York (2001).
Thorburn, D. "Feminism Meets International Relations", 20 *SAIS Review*, No.2, pp. 3–4.
Tickner, J. A. and Sjoberg, G. "Feminism" in T Dunne, M Kurki and S Smith (eds.) *International Relations Theories—Discipline and Diversity*, latest edition, Oxford, Oxford University Press at 180 (2016).
UNDP. The Future We Want: Rights and Empowerment—UNDP Gender Equality Strategy, 2014–2017 (2014).
Uvin, P. "Development Aid and Conflict: Reflections from the Case of Rwanda", Working paper 24, *UN University World Institute for Development Economics Research*, Helsinki (1994).
Vaccero, J. M. "The Politics of Genocide: Peace-Keeping and Disaster Relief in Rwanda" in W J Durch (ed.) in *UN Peace-Keeping, American Policy and the Uncivil Wars of the 1990s*, New York, St Martin's Press (1996) at 369.
Vedross, A. "Quasi-international Agreements and International Economic Transactions", 18 *Year Book of International Affairs* (1964) at 230.
Walters, F. P. *A History of the League of Nations*, London, Oxford University Press (1952).
Zartman, D. W. and Touval, S. (eds.). "International Co-operation: The Extents and Limits of Multilateralism", Cambridge, Cambridge University Press (2010).

Decided Cases and Arbitral Awards

S S "Wimbledon" Great Britain v Germany (PCIJ) (1923) Series A No. 1.
Territorial Jurisdiction of the International Commission of the River Oder, PCIJ (1929) Series A No. 23.
Nuclear Test Cases, ICJ Reports (1974) at 253.
Tinoco Arbitration (1923) UNRIAA 369.
Klein v Republic of Austria, Annual Digest (1948) Case No 18.
Dass v Secretary of State for India in Council (1875) LR 19.
Sedco Inc Iranian Oil Co and the Islamic Republic of Iran, Iran-US claims Tribunal, Awards of 24 October 1985, 27 March 1986 and 2 July 1989, 84 *International Law Reports* (1991) 484.
Mobil Oil Iran Inc and Others v Government of the (Islamic Republic of Iran and the National Iranian Oil Co and Others v Government of the Islamic Republic of Iran and National Iranian Oil Co., Award No 311–74/76/81/150–3), 86 *International Law Reports* (1991) 231.
Chile v France (The Grano Case), UN Report, vol. xv at 77.

The Schooner Exchange v McFaddon, Supreme Court of the United States (1812) (7 Cranch) 116.
The Cristina [1934] AC 485.
The Parlement Belge (1880) LR 5 PD 197.
Porto Alexandre [1920] P 30.
Duff Development Company v Kelantan [1924] AC 797.
Alfred Dunhill of London Inc v Republic of Cuba, 15 International Legal Materials, 1976 at 735.
Trendtex Trading Corporation Ltd v Central Bank of Nigeria [1977] 2 WLR 356.
1o Congreso Del Partido [1981] 2 ALL ER 1064.
Alcom Ltd v Republic of Colombia [1984] 2 ALL ER 6.
Davis Contractors Ltd v Fareham UDC [1986] AC 696 at 729.
Metropolitan Water Board v Dick Kerr & Co [1918] AC 119 at 139.
Austro-German Customs Regime, PCIJ Series A/B No. 41 (1931) at 47.
The Ambatielos Case (Preliminary Objections) ICJ Reports (1952) at 28 and 40.
Certain Expenses of the United Nations, ICJ Reports (1962) at 151.

UN Documents

The Convention on the Elimination of All Forms of Discrimination Against Women, New York, UN Treaty Collection (2017) https://www.un.org/womenwatch/daw/cedaw/.
UNDP, The Future We Want: Rights and Empowerment: UNDP Gender Equality Strategy, 2014–2017 at 3 www.undp.org › gender › GenderEqualityStrategy2014-17.
———, Human Development Report, 2016, Human Development for Everyone, New York (2016) at 46 hdr.undp.org.
———, UN Agenda to End Poverty by 2030; Human Development Report (2016) hdr.undp.org › en › content.
UNICEF, At Least 65,000 Children Released From Armed Forces and Groups over the Last 10 Years—UNICEF News Release, New York and Paris (2017) https://www.unicef.org/press-releases/least-65000-children-released-armed-forces-and-groups-over-last-10-years-unicef.
UNTS (UN Treaty Series)—The Peace Treaty with Italy, 1947, vol. 49 at 126 treaties.un.org.

Index[1]

[1] Note: Page numbers followed by 'n' refer to notes.

C. Chatterjee, *Negotiating Techniques in Diplomacy and Business Contracts*, https://doi.org/10.1007/978-3-030-81732-9

The manufacturer's authorised representative in the EU is Springer Nature Customer Service Centre GmbH, Europaplatz 3, 69115 Heidelberg, Germany. If you have any concerns regarding our products, please contact ProductSafety@springernature.com

Printed and bound by CPI Group (UK) Ltd, Croydon, CR0 4YY
30/09/2026
02225466-0017